POST-RITA REFLECTIONS

A Sociological Journey

Stan Weeber

Hamilton Books
A member of
The Rowman & Littlefield Publishing Group
Lanham · Boulder · New York · Toronto · Plymouth, UK

Copyright © 2009 by
Hamilton Books
4501 Forbes Boulevard
Suite 200
Lanham, Maryland 20706
Hamilton Books Acquisitions Department (301) 459-3366

Estover Road
Plymouth PL6 7PY
United Kingdom

Library of Congress Control Number: 2008936232
ISBN-13: 978-0-7618-4374-0 (paperback : alk. paper)
ISBN-10: 0-7618-4374-4 (paperback : alk. paper)
eISBN-13: 978-0-7618-4375-7
eISBN-10: 0-7618-4375-2

Contents

Preface

Sociologists are sometimes counterintuitive when it comes to human tragedy and disaster. They may act in the strangest ways at the most inopportune times. Once the immediate, raw emotion of the horrific event has passed, the sociologist may entertain the thought that "this is a terrific opportunity to do research," at the risk of appearing seriously off base to all in his or her presence.

I can remember very well what happened in my home town, just a few blocks from where I attended elementary school in Iowa City. On the afternoon of November 22, 1963, University of Iowa researchers walked door to door to measure their neighbors' reactions to one of the most extraordinary, unforeseen and shocking events of the twentieth century, the assassination of John F. Kennedy. Often that afternoon, more than a few normally well mannered Iowans slammed their doors in the faces of the researchers, feeling that it was not a very good time to do research.

The qualitative research and reflections presented in this book could be interpreted much the same way. It could appear to be an insensitive narrative account of unspeakable tragedy suffered in southwestern Louisiana, and thus highly inappropriate. But there are reasons for carrying it out anyway. Disasters such as Hurricane Rita put social institutions to the test and press all of our socially learned civil behaviors to the very limit. By studying disasters we get knowledge for knowledge sake—the limits to which institutions can stretch as well as the limits on civility—as well information that might make future disasters less painful for those that suffer them. At a personal level, the processing of our own experience may be a form of therapeutically reliving the bad event; at least that is true in my case. And finally, Rita as a "forgotten storm" needs to be remembered. It caused too much damage physically, emotionally and culturally for society simply to forget about it.

The approach I utilize in remembering Hurricane Rita is called sociological storytelling. What is this and how is it different from a simple biographical account of a disastrous event?

A biographical account is someone's tale of their Hurricane Rita experience. It may be especially exciting or well told, though skill in story telling is not a requirement. The words are powerful, however, as the experience is framed in the lexicon of one who experienced the even first hand. Literally thousands of such accounts have been published in an archive of 2005 hurricane stories published by the Smithsonian Institution, George Mason University and the University of New Orleans. For historians in particular, this will be a rich vein of information about the hurricanes and how people coped or didn't. Some of the essays in this book were originally published in draft form in this archive. Due to this database, Hurricanes Katrina and Rita are likely to become the most studied hurricanes in history.

In contrast, sociological storytelling is a story informed by sociology. Using Mills' classic "sociological imagination" as a guide, the story is about how lived experience is structured by social contexts. In the telling of my Rita experiences, my own biography is intertwined with the historical period in which I live, the historical event I endured and also the social structure in which I live. Thus, it is not just my story but may apply or have some generalizability to the lived experience of hurricane evacuees in a post-Katrina era. The era is one in which the resources to draw on in times of emergency are very unequally distributed or skewed in an immoral way toward those who possess an important quantity called "social capital." In other words, the rich or the better off, with their elaborate social networks, fared better than the poor and had happier stories to tell. For this reason, the account might be of interest to sociologists, political scientists, historians, politicians, policy analysts, and citizens of southwestern Louisiana who want to read an account that might validate or question much of what they themselves went through during and after Hurricane Rita.

Sociological storytelling also adopts a narrative style in which the writing reveals the process by which the writer has arrived at his or her thoughts, lets readers in on personal doubts, makes the writer vulnerable in the text, and reflects on roads taken and not taken. If this book is to be value to others, it must open a window to the thought processes that accompanied the substantial leap that I was able to make from sociologist to evacuee and back to sociologist. It was a nonlinear, difficult, and insecure road full of nightmarish roadblocks and fear of what might transpire next.

As this is written, there are signs of life in the places most completely destroyed by Hurricane Rita. Restaurants and other businesses are opening in Cameron and Creole, Louisiana. In nearby Oak Grove, new graves provide shiny new resting places for caskets washed away by Rita. About sixty families have returned to Holly Beach, some in trailers, others in newly constructed homes built to a stricter building code—they are fifteen to twenty feet off the ground in many cases. The new bright red roof at Johnson Bayou High School signals a bold new beginning for students there. About 95 percent of Sabine Pass, Texas in far southeastern Texas is rebuilt and the town appears, outwardly at least, to have survived the latest in a long string of hurricanes. The town's Firehouse Number 4, fresh from its *Extreme Makeover* experience, stands ready to serve. In Lake Charles, people are buying up or returning to homes abandoned after Rita, and a certain sense of normalcy has been restored. However, not all of the physical and mental scars have been healed. For some, they may never heal. Having your town physically and socially rearranged for you against your will is among life's most unpleasant experiences and among the worst things that human beings can endure. I am now convinced that the events told in this book cannot be completely appreciated unless you have been through something like this yourself.

My choice of the main title for this book was influenced by one of my favorite writers, Brad Goins, whose initial newspaper column after Rita bore a similar title. Goins is a gem of a writer, popular in southwest Louisiana but I suspect not well known beyond the nearby parishes that read his employer's regional paper, *Lagniappe*. In his memorable post Rita piece, he skillfully wove his own hurricane narrative into an assessment of what needed to be done after the storm. Neither wildly optimistic nor pessimistic or fatalistic, Goins' column provided a steady hand that soothed the nerves of southwest Louisianans as they began to pick up the pieces after Rita. Admirably, he gave credit to local leaders such as Randy Roach who were trying to interest the national media in what was happening in Cameron. And, Goins and his paper did not forget Cameron as much of America did. To most of the national media, Cameron Parish was the forgotten place of the forgotten storm.

The 2006 hurricane season was thankfully mild. The next year, a one-day event named Hurricane Humberto reminded us that the volatility in the Gulf was real and that it would just be a matter of time before disaster strikes us again.

A new hurricane season in the Gulf lurks close by. In a few days, the 2008 Atlantic hurricane season begins, and it is supposed to be a busy one along the Atlantic and the Gulf of Mexico. A medical professional I interviewed said that another storm of the magnitude of Katrina or Rita—should it strike Louisiana, will leave in its wake not only broken homes and lives, but also a mental health crisis that is beyond our ability to imagine. For that reason more than any other, I am hoping and praying that no such tragedy occurs for anyone living along the usual corridors in which hurricanes travel.

Stan Weeber
Lake Charles, Louisiana
May 30, 2008

Acknowledgments

I had no idea where to begin in thanking all those who helped my family during and after Hurricane Rita struck southwest Louisiana in September of 2005. One way to proceed would be to start by thanking people "chronologically," in the order in which assistance was rendered. For every person mentioned I'm quite sure there are at least twenty that I neglected to thank. With that as preamble, and realizing that this acknowledgment is imperfect at best, let the thanking begin.

I was extremely grateful to Mr. Walter Brown, Presiding Overseer of the Christian Congregation of Jehovah's Witnesses in Farmerville, Louisiana for shepherding my family during this difficult time. A simple thank you is of course inadequate to portray the breadth and depth of the help that was given to us. Our refrigerator was full, but more important, our social and spiritual needs were fully attended to in the finest possible manner. A member of this congregation, Pamela Walker, unselfishly offered us an apartment as well as her home, and this is a debt which cannot be repaid. Every member of the congregation contributed in some way to our well being during our crisis, and the value of this assistance to my family has no numerical or dollar referent.

Dr. Steve Unkel, a Farmerville physician, showed exceptional hospitality to the storm weary strangers who rudely interrupted his already busy schedule. His sons, Danny and Steven, evacuated from Lake Charles with my family and provided much needed guidance and support during our evacuation and for months beyond.

We were grateful to the Mayor of Farmerville, Willie Davis, and to the Union Parish Red Cross Shelter which attended to the needs of Katrina evacuees first, and then to Rita survivors. Our thanks as well go to the librarians and staff of the

Farmerville Public Library who graciously served the informational needs of evacuees from two storms and also one moody sociologist who spent way more time than was necessary inside their library.

Back in Lake Charles, I appreciated the steady, level headed leadership of Mayor Randy Roach and the essays of Brad Goins, who helped us all remain sane after Rita tore up our city. At McNeese State, I appreciated the task force that put our wrecked school back into order, including President Robert Hebert, Provost Jeanne Daboval, Dean of Liberal Arts Ray Miles, and Head of Social Sciences, Billy Turner. Dr. Turner put on a clinic on how to put a collegiate department back into order after a disaster: by allowing his veteran staff the space to create their own academic spheres after the storm without micromanaging any of us. Again all these efforts are acknowledged but cannot be repaid.

The friends I met at the memorable 2006 meetings of the Southern Sociological Society in New Orleans encouraged me to tell my story because they thought that it was important. I owe a huge debt of gratitude to Danielle Hidalgo, Kristen Barber, Jessica Pardee, Andrea Wilbon, Tim Haney, Jennifer Day and April Brayfield for validating my work. The audience in attendance at that remarkable session in New Orleans was great beyond words, especially all who spoke with us individually after the session was over to give their condolences for all we lost during the two storms.

My raw, uncut stories after Katrina and Rita were first published in the Hurricane Digital Memory Bank at the University of New Orleans, and I am grateful to Dr. Michael Mizell-Nelson, Assistant Professor of History at UNO and the Content and Outreach Lead for the Hurricane Digital Memory Bank for allowing my voice to be heard. His valuable assistance lead to the creation of a McNeese State subcollection within the memory bank where the McNeese stories could be compiled and heard. We are still in the middle of this project; we hope we finish it before the next storm comes. Additionally and most gratefully, I am thankful to Dr. Mizell-Nelson for his help in promoting this book; I can only hope that I will be able to reciprocate this assistance some day.

Several editors found my sociological stories after Katrina and Rita to be of interest. My sincerest and heartfelt thanks go to Duane Gill, Danielle Hidalgo, Kristen Barber, Barbara Stover Gingerich, John Troesser, Debi Orton and John Cross for entertaining the idea that a sociological story, unscientific as it might appear to others, has intrinsic as well as extrinsic value.

For the third time, University Press of America, parent company of Hamilton Books, has taken on a project of mine and I'm pleased to report that our relationship is stronger than ever—a grand accomplishment indeed for such a long term relationship. Once again I am very grateful to UPA Vice President Judith Rothman for seeing the value of my work and giving it a voice, this time with Hamilton Books.

Behind the scenes, more people than I will ever know worked hard to get this book done and to get it out on time: production personnel, editors, and their assistants labored hard for many hours on my behalf. This is my second project with UPA Acquisitions Editor Patti Belcher and I've especially enjoyed the positive attitude that she brings to her work.

My "family of evacuation" at the old Burton Street house in Lake Charles— my wife Julie Weeber, my daughter Abigail Westby and my niece Holly Featherstone (now Holly Unkel) deserve much credit for surviving my post-hurricane irritability and for allowing more space than I needed to construct the sociological stories (at first, sociological rants) that ultimately became the chapters of this book. Holly's father Fred Featherstone risked his life to give us the critical information that every evacuee needs, and later provided me with valuable and much needed research assistance in preparing individual chapters of this book.

Speaking of family, our extended families deserve a warm salute for their ongoing concern and support. The Weebers clustered near Iowa City as well as the chronically dispersed Featherstones gave material and emotional support beyond the call of duty.

Finally, the medal for "long suffering," goes to my wife and to my daughter. This is the tenth book length project they have endured with good cheer and smiles. If I could find such a medal I would provide it; but alas, like the other massive debts accumulated during this project, it will probably have to remain unpaid, and for this I apologize.

Chapter 1

Hurricane Rita and Aftermath

This chapter is the narrative story of how my family and I survived Hurricanes Katrina and Rita and their aftermaths from August, 2005 through May, 2008. The story is punctuated with sociological musings and observations, as the writings of many sociologists came to mind during the long and worrisome experience of watching the storms develop in the Gulf, and after Rita, evacuating, relocating, waiting, returning, and readjusting to the new life that awaited me upon my return to Lake Charles, Louisiana and McNeese State, where I teach sociology.

Initially I chose the chapter title "Beating The Storms," because of the positive outcome that my family experienced. We beat the two storms, Katrina and Rita. We survived with our good health and good humor intact. Our home in Lake Charles received only minor damage during Rita. A vehicle we left behind was unharmed. With the assistance we received from FEMA, the Red Cross and the State of Louisiana, my family's meager finances actually improved a bit after the hurricane. We have Hurricane Katrina to thank for being alive today because it caused us to be vigilant and to get out of harm's way as Rita approached.

My own sense of personal optimism was tempered as I began to hear the stories of others whose situations were less fortunate than my own. Many of our friends in southern Louisiana did not beat the storms at all. The catastrophic pictures from New Orleans spoke volumes about the diaspora experienced by hundreds of thousands who lost everything that they owned in the storm, and who may or may not return to the city. After Rita, we knew of many families in southwest Louisiana whose homes were unlivable. Our friends in Cameron Parish (to the south of Lake Charles closer to the Gulf) faced a long and difficult period of displacement. The coastal town of Cameron sustained catastrophic damage and the nearby resort town of Holly Beach was basically blown off the face of the earth by Rita. This was the kind of damage that Katrina left in New Orleans and in south Mississippi. I feel intense emotional pain for those whose losses were overwhelming. Therefore, I agree with Danielle Hidalgo when she states that storytelling is a sociological process that allows for healing but also provides a space for wounds and pain that cannot be cured but only endured.[1]

Hurricane Katrina

The effects of Katrina felt in Lake Charles were more social than physical, at least at first. As the storm blew through on August 29, 2005 Lake Charles, on the far western edge of the storm, experienced only a brief afternoon shower. By the next day, social waves from Katrina were felt here. The third floor of our Teacher Education building at McNeese had been converted into a special needs shelter for people evacuated from New Orleans. After a day or two, the shelter was shifted to the Recreation Building. In addition, our winter sports venue, Burton Coliseum, was opened to busloads of evacuees that were now streaming in. Then, we began to see the first of about 200 college students from New Orleans who had enrolled on an emergency basis to continue their educations at McNeese State. We welcomed the new students, extending our late registration for the fall semester, raising the enrollment limits in some classes, and keeping a close eye on the students to monitor any physical or mental health issues that they may be facing.

Rumors quickly spread that Katrina evacuees in Baton Rouge, Lake Charles, and other towns were hijacking cars, robbing businesses, and fomenting riots.[2] These rumors were mostly untrue but caused a wave of angst among the locals. Natural disasters and their aftermaths tend to be breeding grounds for rumor according to the sociology of disaster literature.[3]

Hurricane Rita

As Tropical Storm Rita became the 17th named storm of the 2005 season on Sunday, September 18, the news produced no particular concern in Louisiana. Early models had it delivering a glancing blow to the Florida Keys and then after that, a westward plunge into the Gulf of Mexico. In a record year for hurricane production, it became just one more storm to watch. Most of the time, people in Louisiana are not looking hard at any storm until it reaches the warm waters of the Gulf.

I felt fairly secure living in Southwest Louisiana. Audrey was a devastating storm, but it had occurred long ago, in 1957. In 2002 there was a near miss with Lily. It made landfall near New Iberia, and the bad weather spun off of it reached within 10 miles of Lake Charles but left us virtually untouched. In between those hurricanes there had not been very much major storm activity along the coast directly to our south. A hurricane landfall map that I consulted (pre-Rita) showed a section of the Southwest Louisiana coast from Cameron to just west of New Iberia that had never experienced a major hurricane landfall. Looking at the map, it was about the only bare spot I could find on a map that was basically filled by brown dots that represented storms that had hit the Gulf Coast from Brownsville, Texas to Miami, Florida.

Tuesday, September 20: Just before starting a "test review" session at my 8 A.M. Sociological Theory class, I announce that the forthcoming test, the first of the semester, would be held the following Thursday, the 22nd, "weather permitting." Little did I know then that the class would take this test on Thursday, November 10, seven weeks from the originally planned test date.

Wednesday, September 21: At 8 AM, I have just completed handing out a test to an early morning section of Introductory Sociology students. For many of these freshmen, it is their first college test. Despite the hurricane looming in the Gulf, attendance was good. The fear of God is still in these youngsters, I reasoned, because the college experience is new to them. I sternly watched from my podium at the front of the room. Today, this was not to prevent cheating but only to give off the impression of looking for cheaters.[4] I hoped that the stern expression might in itself be a form of deterrence. As I looked vacantly at the students from my perch in the front, the question that weighed heaviest on my mind was not about who was cheating or who wasn't, but this: where will my family be this weekend?

After hours of rumors, the official word finally reaches me at 1:30 P.M. that school is cancelled on Thursday and Friday. Wednesday's night classes will go on as scheduled. As of this afternoon, Lake Charles is on the edge of the "cone of uncertainty" of several computerized hurricane tracking models, which means that we were not anticipating a direct hit, but could experience significant wind and rain from a landfall somewhere on the upper Texas Gulf Coast.

The displaced students from New Orleans were very frightened about Rita. A portion of their city was still under water and the broken levees were patched up but not yet repaired. Flood water was being pumped out but the process was very slow. Being hit by Rita would mean more water cascading over the broken levees, and a double dose of misery for the Crescent City.

At 3 P.M., the school announced that Saturday's football game with Northwestern Oklahoma State was cancelled. Immediately I began to grasp to enormous economic costs of the hurricane season to this point. McNeese's game with

Southern University had been cancelled due to Katrina, and now this. Football is one of the key income producers of the college, and this second cancellation was obviously leaving the Athletic Director and other administrators worried about what effect the shortfall in revenue would have upon the athletics budget and the general fund.

At 4 P.M., I go home to poll my family on what their wishes are in the event that a voluntary evacuation is announced. Despite Rita being upgraded to a Category 3 storm, the vote is unanimous: we are going to stay and ride it out.

My Wednesday night class had to go on, so I dutifully reported at 5:25 P.M. with copies of the review sheet for Test 1 for my class in Collective Behavior and Social Movements. I told them that the test would be next Wednesday, September 28, "weather permitting." When the students finally caught up to this test on November 16th, the class had been changed into a distance learning class and the test had been transformed into a "take home" test.

I stumbled badly during the test review on the evening of September 21st, admittedly being distracted by the storm and the fact that some students were whining about having to attend the class—they needed supplies and the stores were running out of them. Worse, I had forgotten my review notes. I left them in the office, and had to give the entire review from memory, which was not a problem but required more concentration to the review than if I had my usual refresher notes.

My mind was racing not only to remember the facts of my review but also to ponder who was not there for the class. Two new students from New Orleans had just entered the class. They had been displaced by Katrina and now would end up having to evacuate a second time. Taking no chances, they were already on their way out of town. Their double evacuee experience may have been, possibly, an historic event in the annals of American academe. I also thought about McNeese State baseball player Tommy Stone who was a student in the class. His parents in St. Bernard Parish had lost everything during Katrina, and he was still tending to their needs and those of whomever needed help in his hometown. His dad, the fire chief for the Parish, was a media favorite who had become a local celebrity for his outspoken criticism of the slowness of the federal response to Katrina.[5] Obviously, Tommy was absent from the review. This young man is an unsung hero of Hurricane Katrina's aftermath. The review was finished by 6:45, and as I dismissed class I told students I'd see them in a week provided all went well with the hurricane.

Evacuation

Thursday, September 22: By 7:30 A.M., I was enjoying the day off from the usual working grind when the *Weather Channel* offered up something that caused some concern. During the evening, the storm had turned in a more northerly direction than anticipated. Folks in Houston and Galveston were sighing with relief, but people in Port Arthur, Orange, Lake Charles, and New Orleans were getting more concerned by the minute as they appeared to be more in the path than before. A mandatory evacuation was announced for the southern half of Calcasieu Parish where the elevation was seven feet above sea level or lower. The evacuation line was only a few miles to the south of my home at this moment.

By 8 A.M. I learned just how quickly things can change with a hurricane approaching. Now, the mandatory evacuation came down for everyone in the parish south of Interstate 10. We were only about two miles south of the Interstate, and my initial reaction was to stay put. However, we got a full dose of peer pressure to pack up and go. All of our neighbors were packing up; then, our landlord came to announce that we must leave as he and his entire family was leaving.[6] That made it official: we were going to leave under the mandatory evacuation order, whether I liked it or not.

At 9 A.M. my family was treading new ground. I had never had to leave my home under such circumstances, nor had any member of my family been displaced by such an event. I had lived in Houston and Galveston from 1988-1994, and I survived several tropical storms and two hurricanes. These storms did not even disrupt daily life; I reported to work as usual. When Lily hit New Iberia, Louisiana in 2002, I stayed behind in Lake Charles under voluntary evacuation and sent my family to Denton, Texas, far out of harm's way. My wife viewed it as a road trip and an opportunity to see old friends. I was extremely naïve in staying behind because I did not know how bad the storm could have been. This was before Katrina.

The phone rings at 9:20; we have been offered a two bedroom apartment in Farmerville, Louisiana. I had no idea where this place was, and would only later in the day have a faint idea of it being near Monroe, in northeastern Louisiana. A friend of ours had arranged this gift, and though he described the apartment as "stark" and lacking amenities—it was a garage apartment with no furniture that had not been lived in for years—we were glad to have somewhere to go and not to have to pay anything out of pocket for it.

We were expecting to form a caravan to Farmerville at noon, but there was a glitch in our plans. One of the cars in our 4-car caravan had an unexpected stop to make that would take some time; and after a period of negotiation, the driver of the 4th car decided to travel alone without aid of the caravan. That being decided, we left with three cars: the lead vehicle was the family friend who arranged the apartment (he is a native of Farmerville), followed by my family's two cars. My wife and I were in one car while my daughter and my niece (both lived with us) were in the second car. It was 1:30 P.M.

We benefited greatly from the road knowledge and street smarts that the lead driver had of the terrain that we were going to travel. Because he had traveled to Farmerville many times, he knew very well the roads that ran north and east out of Lake Charles. He knew that there could be congestion on these roads, even in the best of circumstances. Today, we faced an incredible traffic jam as Calcasieu and Cameron Parishes had been ordered to evacuate by the afternoon. This is

195,000 people. I am quite sure that the fear of Katrina and Katrina like devastation was what motivated so many to comply with the evacuation order. The sociology of disaster literature suggests that people adhere to warnings if they can see physical evidence of what kind of danger they are going to face.[7] The nightly images of New Orleans under water were enough motivation for us to leave.

It was pretty much bumper to bumper traffic to get to the Interstate and then it was still "slow and go" for about the first 10 miles east on I-10. After that, our speed increased to 40 and then to a more normal pace of 55-65 M.P.H.

The lead driver, a bachelor in his late 20s, was not accustomed to traveling with other people. He had to be persuaded to stop for rest breaks, but thankfully he complied.

The first of these stops was in Crowley, Louisiana. At a Shop Rite (convenience store) off I-10, the scene was crowded and loud but orderly. Just about every parking spot in the modest parking lot was filled, and people were stopping at nearby businesses and walking to the Shop Rite. Everyone in the store appeared to be evacuees. After a brief break, we decided to get going again. The headline of the local paper read, "Rita Now A Category 5 Monster." Even though the whole situation was uncomfortable at best, we felt like we made the right choice.

About 5:30 P.M. we exited Interstate 49 in a little town called LeCompte. We were unable to see much of the town because we were stopping for food and fuel and that was it. We entered a Burger King where the scene was much like that in Crowley: loud, crowded, but orderly. The restaurant was packed with evacuees, most from Lake Charles. The atmosphere was still upbeat, and though there were concerned looks on some peoples' faces, there was some laughter and gaiety as well.

At 7:30 we stopped in a little town along U.S. 165 between Alexandria and Monroe. I have no idea of the name of the town despite pondering several maps for about an hour in the days after stopping there. We turned in to the parking lot of a local convenience store on the magnitude of the Shop Rite in Crowley but not part of any chain. The scene was the same as before (Crowley) except that now, people were milling about and willing to talk, and there were some open emotions being displayed; a sobbing woman that spoke with my wife feared that her Lake Charles trailer would be blown away in the storm. I was out of contact with the news (a strange situation for me because I'm a news hound) but the buzz at the convenience store was that Lake Charles might take a direct hit from a Category 5 storm which would basically level the town with a catastrophic wind and water surge. After restarting the caravan, I tried to get some news on the radio about the storm, but to no avail.

When we took our final major turn of the night, on to Louisiana Highway 2 toward Farmerville, my family let out a collective groan. The town was still 18 miles away. We had been led to believe that it was just a few miles outside Monroe.

At 10 P.M. we reached Farmerville, Louisiana and although weary from the upheaval of the day's events, we were ecstatic to have a place to stay. The caravan leader spoke briefly with his father at his father's house before leading us the last few blocks to the place on Academy Street that would be our home for the next two weeks and two days. At 11 o'clock we turned in for some much needed bed rest; and though thankful to our hosts, we asked not to be disturbed until about noon the next day. This was something I'd noticed about the Katrina evacuees in Lake Charles: they were not afraid or shy about advocating for themselves, at one point objecting to our use of the term "refugee" to refer to them. Now the shoe was on the other foot, and we were advocating for ourselves as vigorously as we could.

Friday, September 23: There is no more helpless feeling for an addicted "news hound" than to be shut out of the news, but that was my plight this morning. Rita was near Louisiana, but I had no information at all. There was no news of the storm anywhere. There was no TV in the donated apartment. I tried the portable radio we had brought along with us: nothing. I did not know anyone in the small town well enough to intrude upon their privacy by asking them to look at their TV. I was stuck with no news, and that was it. My family did not appear to want to know any details. They did not want to talk about the storm and appeared to crave only distractions and diversions. I knew that our hosts were struggling financially and I did not ask to watch their TV, realizing they every appliance that was turned on contributed to their electric bill.

At 11 A.M. we received an orientation to our new home and to Deb Walker's home at Academy Street, which we would also use extensively during our stay. Deb's house was huge, making our Lake Charles rental look tiny in comparison. My family appears to be swept up in the enormity of the place, and we all took hot baths there as we had no hot water in the nearby garage apartment. This appeared to be the perfect diversion for my family, who wanted to know nothing of the impending disaster along the Gulf Coast of Louisiana.

Around noon, the Farmerville High School homecoming parade started in front of the Walker's home on Academy and this only continued the ongoing state of detachment and denial from what was happening in the Gulf. This "head in the sand" approach continued on for the afternoon and early evening as friends of the Walkers dropped by to donate supplies for our apartment and to make even more offers of assistance. This small town generosity, lacking in Lake Charles, was a refreshing experience for us.

At 6:30, an elder representing the Farmerville congregation of Jehovah's Witnesses stopped by. This small Christian organization has a largely understated but highly effective disaster relief program for its members, and we belonged to a congregation in Lake Charles. The elder conducted a "needs assessment" very similar to what a social worker might do, with an emphasis on making sure that my family's immediate needs were being met. He recommended that we reach out to take advantage of all the community resources available, especially FEMA. I followed up and contacted FEMA online within an hour of this meeting. Before signing off, I read an Internet weather site that was predicting a 10 foot storm surge in downtown Lake Charles. If this prediction comes true, only the roof of our home will be above water after the storm passes.

The Great Unknown

Saturday, September 24: I remember this morning only because of the dread that I experienced, and I would title it as "the horror of the great unknown." The storm had already passed through Lake Charles but I could not find any information at all at our apartment. Radio stations had no news. Outside, an outer band of Rita unleashed tropical storm force gale winds and showers that only made me feel more nervous. If it's this bad here, in north Louisiana, I could only speculate about what Lake Charles looked like at that moment.

About 11 A.M., the congregation elder stopped by to show me the way to the Union Parish Red Cross shelter just within the city limits. After I parked my car in the Red Cross lot and we shook hands, the man left and I was facing the reality of our evacuation alone for the first time. As I registered at the front desk, a lump appeared in my throat and it was difficult to speak. The urge to cry was there but I suppressed it. I recall this moment as the pinnacle of helplessness. After registering, I presented a Red Cross official with a list of supplies that my family needed, mostly toiletry items; and a staffer promptly went away to fetch the items. Lunch was being served, so I got in line.

As I was getting in line, a volunteer at the shelter introduced herself and gave me a message to relay back to the elder. I readily agreed to do so, tactfully putting aside the thought that this was an imposition upon someone who had possibly lost all their possessions in a hurricane. Later, after much rest and afterthought, I realized it was probably good to ground myself in my new situation and to forget about my worries for a while. In that sense, this encounter was therapeutic.

After lunch, I watched CNN at the shelter and finally got some news about what had happened. The station reported that the hurricane was a Category 2 when it hit Lake Charles, and that there was no major flooding. I instantly began to feel a bit better. This was not going to be Katrina like devastation. A stronger hurricane would have carried the predicted storm surge, plus the flattening effect of several hours of winds over 100 miles per hour. In lesser hurricanes the damage is more sporadic and not quite as catastrophic. I went to our garage apartment, rounded up my family and took them back to the shelter, telling them only that it was less than a "Katrina" punch that had hit Lake Charles. They still showed little interest in the gory details, not even wanting to look at the television at the shelter. After lunch we headed back toward town with our Red Cross supplies and some contentment after having been well fed.

We stopped off at a former video store that had been converted by the Red Cross and the National Guard into a clothing depot for evacuees. We flashed our evacuee nametags to the Guardsmen at the door; then, they offered us water and soft drinks. After that, we could simply take our time wandering through the store and take our pick, for free, of any clothing that fit. My blood pressure was starting to go down as I realized that I would have a few changes of clothes while staying in Farmerville.

Enlightenment

My niece's cell phone rang; it was her father (Freddie, my brother in law). Incredibly, he had made the trip from his home in San Antonio to Lake Charles in the early morning hours just after the storm passed through, braving the huge I-10 bridge over Lake Charles which was still swaying in gale force winds. He wanted to check on our rental house and on his daughter's pets (a hamster, lizard, fish, and bird) that could not be evacuated. He happily reported that the pets were just fine and the house was OK except for a few lost shingles and a window blown out of the storage shed in the back.

This is the exact news that every evacuee wants to know from the moment that the storm has passed through his or her town. We were extremely fortunate to have received it less than 12 hours after the storm passed through. Some of the Katrina evacuees had to wait a month or more to find out what happened to their homes. We got our news days or weeks in advance of the time that other Rita evacuees got theirs; the "look and leave" phase for Calcasieu Parish began September 30, and many had no way of traveling back to see what had transpired at their homes.[8] Cameron Parish residents would have to wait months before being allowed back to "look and leave."

With this news, the mood of our group lightened. We felt very fortunate, even blessed. Now, my thoughts immediately turned to how quickly I could return to work. I love my job and I'm not sure how I ever got along before I became a sociology professor. I knew that for each school day missed, there would be a consequence for the students in my classes. Then there were the research and writing projects in progress that were collecting dust in my office. I was very anxious to know if they survived the hurricane although I suspected that they had at this point. My office is on the third floor or our building, well beyond any possible storm surge but the roof was old and rickety, and I feared some kind of water leakage into my office.

About 2 P.M. in the afternoon, I got a reality check about what was going on in Lake Charles. A FOX news crew, apparently reacting to the CNN report of "no major flooding," went to the Lake Charles boardwalk area just off the lake and very close to the downtown area of Lake Charles. The crew was floating in a boat in a storm surge of about five feet of water near the downtown boardwalk. Some familiar areas to us, including the shelter on the lake where my wife and I ate lunch on Labor Day, were now under water. A new wave of concern came over me. Was this storm surge part of the original storm or did it come in during one of the strong bands of wind and rain that accompany hurricanes? It could be a surge that hit town after my brother in law left. To remain calm, I just continued to keep reiterating what my brother in law Freddie told us: no standing water anywhere near our home. I just had to believe that that was the case and that nothing had changed after he left town. Still, I was back to a situation where I was worried, and badly needed to look and see for myself what kind of damage there was at our home.

Waiting, Wondering, Thinking, Musing

At our congregation meeting the next morning, Sunday, September 25, the elders checked to see if our needs were being met and cared for. Indeed they were. The previous evening it was necessary for us to tell our new friends that our refrigerator in the apartment was full and that we were not wanting for anything at the moment. We relayed the good news to many about our Lake Charles home and expressed our relief as well as appreciation for all that people had done for us. When the elders asked if I had a projected date for returning, I told them only that I would like to return about two days before classes began, and I was estimating this to be October 1st.

Week of September 25: I spent my days at the Farmerville Public Library where I worked hard at studying disaster benefits and monitoring events in Lake Charles via Internet. Two professors from Tulane were there, too. The worn, exhausted look on their faces bore the pressure of the uncertainty of their own diasporas. We exchanged sympathetic glances but that was all we could muster in terms of communication. Meanwhile, my family's bank account was running low and in need of reinforcement. This week we received our FEMA check and also learned that McNeese State was going to pay its employees utilizing Western Union, an innovation that caught the eye of *The Chronicle of Higher Education*[9]. As payday was Friday, I could see that a trip back to Lake Charles to do some banking was in order; also, to check up on our property to see if there had been any storm surge flooding.

The branch bank in Lake Charles was not yet open but the main office in Crowley was; so it was to Crowley that I ventured to get my paycheck via Western Union and then to put it in the bank along with my FEMA check.

The Western Union clerk at the Piggly Wiggly in Crowley will never forget me as long as she lives, I'm sure, and I wondered how many other McNeese faculty and staff would come her way. She was obviously hoping for no more of us to darken her door. She had to go back to her boss' safe three times to get the money for my monthly paycheck; not that I'm highly paid, but Western Union apparently cannot send more than $1,000 in one batch, so it took three batches to finish getting my pay. Both the clerk and I were relieved when it was over.

I took I-10 to Jennings and then opted for the scenic route, U.S. 90 to Lake Charles. There had been reports that I-10 was closed at Lake Charles and that the State Police were not letting people through. The reports were probably untrue but I took them seriously anyway.

The damage increased as I got nearer to Lake Charles. Compared with the trip from Farmerville to Crowley, I could now see more trees down and more structural damage to buildings. Between Welsh and Lacassine, a large telephone pole had been blown over about half of the highway and it was just hanging there, dislodged from its usual base and dangling precariously over the two lanes of traffic. I accelerated to get out from under the pole, praying all the time that it would not fall on me. At Lacassine, there was no power at all; same thing in Iowa, just 10 miles east of Lake Charles.

Entering Lake Charles on Highway 90, the electricity was off, all of the traffic lights were out, and intersections were transformed into four way stops. The damage to the town was sporadic and unpredictable. Some buildings had their roofs peeled off while others appeared to be undamaged; however, this visual test of damage could be deceiving. Though some roofs appeared to have no damage, they could have lost enough shingles so that rain entered the buildings, necessitating blue tarps to be placed on them to prevent further rain from entering, and further water damage. If the tarps did not arrive before the first major rain after Rita, which was in November, then the buildings sustained even more water damage.

Less than half a mile from my home, the Shop Rite/Conoco where my family usually bought gas looked small and barren; the high metal frames or overhangs that kept us out of the rain and sun had blown down and were now a tangled mass of metal debris along the side of the road, waiting to be picked up. Right across the street was an Exxon station, it looked virtually untouched, there was not even any debris strewn about in the parking lot of the station.

Turning right onto Burton Street, I had to be a careful navigator so as to avoid the multiple piles of debris which had been temporarily arranged by someone (neighbors possibly) so as to allow a narrow path down the street. Power lines were down. Further down the block, I could see that some trees had been uprooted. Pulling into my driveway, there was just barely enough room to get a car through. Someone had moved the debris from under our carport; it might have been my brother-in-law Freddie Featherstone or it could have been my neighbor Wes Viator; I'm not sure. In any event, I was just barely able to pull in and get out of the car—no small feat given all the debris that was blown down and around in the street and in yards. This included power lines, tree limbs, leaves, garbage pails and contents, and belongings from other people's houses that had blown onto our property. There had been no flooding on my street, consistent with CNN's reporting.

It was shocking to see everything in such disarray, but at another level of consciousness everything looked OK to me considering the circumstances and the realization that things could have been much, much worse. I had a flashback of a severely flooded neighborhood in New Orleans that I had seen on TV. What I was seeing with my own eyes in Lake Charles was shocking but at the same time far less devastating: an out-building in the back yard had part of the roof blown off, but remarkably, the part of the storage shed that housed our excess belongings had held up. It was mostly a lot of junk that our landlord had discarded that got wet inside the shelter. A window pane was blown out of the door of a second out-building that housed lawn equipment. The screen door on the front door of our house was gone, blown far away, who knows where; but that was OK, we had never liked it anyway. A well mannered thief had drained one half of the gasoline in my niece's truck, leaving the other half for her to use.

The next three days were probably the most miserable that I've ever spent in my life—hot, sweaty, bitten by mosquitoes, without electrical power, and uncertain about the future. I had the unpleasant task of emptying out the rotten and moldy foodstuffs left in the refrigerator; and then threw myself into a series of home improvement tasks, most important of which was the removal of some of the debris from the front lawn and arranging it alongside the curb for the city to pickup. The first day I had no phone; by the second day, I could call out but apparently could not receive any calls. I called my sister in Iowa City and left a message. Also, I tried to phone my wife in Farmerville but could not get through. There was no water pressure, so bathing was out of the question, and I'd have to carry in some water to get the toilet to flush.

There was a Super Wal-Mart open; it was one of the few stores that was up and running. They were open from 9 AM to 4 PM and were staffed with people that they could assemble from "wherever," some of them from far away. I stocked up on water, non-perishable food, and cleaning supplies. Outside, workers were stationed next to a tractor trailer, handing out three bags of ice and three gallons of water per car. The leftover ice that accumulated at home became my bathing water.

The town was a working man's paradise. Hastily-made signs shouted "workers wanted." The kind of work that was needed was menial, to be sure; but I was struck with the thought that it would be a huge opportunity both for the legitimate entrepreneur as well as the innovative deviant or criminal.[10] In the weeks and months after the storm, the working-class population appeared to grow well beyond its pre Rita level, and the increased traffic was testing the demeanor of the most well mannered Acadian. Ironically, hundreds of white collar and office workers had to be laid off due to lack of work. In that sense, the storm had reorganized or reconstituted the town: new people coming in to work; some former residents including about 10 percent of the student body of McNeese did not return; and some returned and then left because they had been laid off.

In New Orleans after Katrina, the population had shrunk, and as a result, portions of the city suffered "panopticon effect"[11] where just about everything was visible because so few were present. There was the suspicion that everyone and everything was being monitored. Sociology graduate students at Tulane also complained of the "masculinization of space" that occurred with the influx of male construction workers, many of whom were Latino. Some wrote of sexual harassment and speculated that there had been rising rates of domestic violence after Katrina.[12]

Certainly there was potential for these problems in Lake Charles, but it was difficult to tell as Lake Charles appeared to have problems more like Baton Rouge, where the population was said to have nearly doubled after Katrina. Among other things, the storm had dispersed many of the state's sexual predators to places unknown. They were required to check in at their new place of residence but many did not. Months after the storm, hundreds of these predators were still on the loose and unaccounted for.[13]

As a sociologist, my thoughts wandered back to the profession that I love, and though my thoughts were unconventional, they offered up a way to process and assimilate my disaster experiences within a framework that made sense to me.[14]

The basic sociological concept I pondered the most during my own evacuee experience was the concept of chance.[15] Only by chance did we in Lake Charles escape a catastrophic situation. Chance thus took on a real life meaning for us that was concrete rather than abstract.

I began to compare how I viewed chance before and after the storm. Before the storm, it was just another sociological concept that I taught to my students, a valued one to be sure, as we believe that our research is better if it takes chance into account. When drawing a sample we feel more comfortable with a random sample (as opposed to a snowball sample) because it does a better job of representing the population we are studying. Everyone has an equal chance of being selected for the survey. We feel even better, once our observations are subject to statistical analysis, if the results show "statistical significance," where the results reported occur within a pattern greater than chance alone would dictate. In both instances we are taking chance occurrences or happenstance out of the equation. The long evacuee experience has a way of reducing these more theoretic thoughts down to a material base: chance is the random violence that a hurricane of Katrina or Rita's magnitude does to your town and to your neighborhood. As Rita entered Lake Charles, described variously as a high level Category 2 storm or a low level Category 3 storm, it skipped around so that some dwellings were totally destroyed while others received no damage at all. Everyone in town now knows that to avoid witnessing such chance occurrences as having your dwelling destroyed, it is better to leave during a hurricane than to stay and ride it out. People in New Orleans that I spoke with feel the same way.

Despite some optimistic moments, I was fighting hard not to be overwhelmed at the damage inflicted by the storm, and I felt creeping insecurity about my school and whether it would reopen. I was wondering if what had happened in New Orleans would also happen here. Schools (including colleges) in New Orleans had closed for the semester after Katrina. In Lake Charles, the original prognosis for McNeese's reopening had been overly optimistic: the initial date of reopening on the McNeese web site indicated a September 29th reopening. This was quickly withdrawn. It happened so fast that I never did see the announcement. The second announcement said the school would reopen October 3rd. At the beginning of my visit home, this was less than a week away.

On the second day in Lake Charles, I was able to make outgoing calls. The first one was to the university's main number, where a woman on tape said that the school was closed indefinitely. Feelings of insecurity and dread came back hard upon me and I feared for the future.

Making my way to the campus, I discovered that it had been taken over by the National Guard and was a major base of regional recovery operations. Despite several signs indicating the campus was closed, I parked near campus and walked to my office building, pretending to be just looking at the damage. The large windows of the McDonald's across the street from my building had been blown out; a portion of the debris was still lingering on Ryan Street. Carefully I slid through the door of my building (it was blown off its hinges) and up to my office. There were standing puddles of water along several sections of the third floor; a smell that resembled an engine overheating; and there was some water driven debris in the hallway just outside my office. Thankfully, there appeared to be no water damage inside of my office, including my computer and printer, and the boxes of data stored on floppy disks. I grabbed a few files of interest and fled, not wanting to be discovered by a Guardsman on patrol. I spent the rest of the day on home improvement projects, taking many breaks from the sweaty work and drinking some of the water I'd brought from Wal-Mart.

Week of October 2: Sunday, October 2nd marked the midway point of my long, hot and uncomfortable visit home. I toiled away at home improvement tasks until overcome by fatigue and sweat, then refreshed myself with cold water. Though the calendar was now turned to October, it was still hot; it was 88 degrees outdoors and also inside my house. The humidity was stifling, and I had to endure the uninvited mosquitoes that held court in my living room when I opened the door. And opening the door was a must, unless I wanted the heat inside the house to rise well above 90 degrees.

During the long breaks between tasks, I thought some more about the randomness of the violence inflicted by the two storms, especially Rita. As I sat on my couch and stared out the open front door there were two houses across the street that from the naked eye, at least, appeared to have no damage whatsoever. There was not even much debris in their yards. The places looked about the same as they did on the day we evacuated. South and north of this little section of no violence there was plenty of it: at the south end of the block, the debris piles along the curb were higher than most cars, and the power lines dangled helplessly from the power poles at that end of Burton Street. North of us, there were two large trees that had been uprooted, and the quiet of the street was interrupted only by the sounds of portable generators and the constant whir of chain saws slowly chewing up the downed trees into smaller, more manageable pieces. I contemplated as well how my street had fared better overall than others about a mile away. Lake Street, a busy north to south thoroughfare on the south side, was completely impassable due to downed power lines, fallen trees, large masses of debris, and flooding. In New Orleans, something similar occurred in that the French Quarter was on high ground and appeared at least to have sustained little damage. Not far from there was the Lower Ninth Ward that would continue to look like a war zone well into the spring of 2008.

My thoughts kept drifting back to sociology. I have been a sociologist since my early days as a Master's student, and because of the accumulated years that sociology has occupied my life, it was hard for my mind to turn away from it, even in the midst of my current difficulties. What I was contemplating was unorthodox to say the least: I pledged never again to take lightly the tests of statistical significance that are used in my discipline. For years I had been a qualitative sociologist who did not have much use for statistics at all. When I worked on quantitative projects, I tended not to take the .05 level of significance very seriously. In the discussion section of the few quantitative papers I wrote, I was always willing to talk about the variables approaching significance as if they were important. Why? I remembered interviewing a psychologist in Texas who was a few months away from retirement after an accomplished career. In a moment of fatigue at the end of a long working day, the 78 year old told me that the way variables are measured and tested in the social sciences is "pretty damned arbitrary," meaning not as exact as we would like, and the conclusions based on the tests are not as solid as we would like them to be.[16] What the distinguished professor said lingered with me for years, and I frankly never took statistical tests of significance very seriously after that.

All that changed after surviving the hurricanes. Between 7:30 and 8:00 AM on the morning of September 22, a computer model deep within the National Oceanographic and Atmospheric Administration was predicting danger for Calcasieu and Cameron Parishes, and did so with at least 95 percent confidence that danger was imminent. Thus the possibility of danger was projected to be significant according to the model. The model turned out to be accurate. Everyone who left was glad that they did; everyone I spoke to that stayed wished they'd left. Those that stayed faced the random wrath of the storm and all the uncertainty and fear that came with a hurricane of that intensity. Because of the large number of people who evacuated, there was no loss of human life in Lake Charles that I know of from the storm. In New Orleans, a similar computer model had generated the mass evacuation of the city before Katrina. Many of those who stayed wished that they had not.

My sociological daydreaming ended when a hopeful sign on the evening of October 2 jolted me back to reality. A truck from an electrical company in Virginia suddenly appeared on Burton Street. The truck made its way partly down the street, and the men stopped, got out and began visually examining the damage to the power lines along the street. After about an hour, they got back in their trucks and moved further down the street. It appeared that they would be finished with this initial examination by nightfall.

The next morning I had a decision to make. I was hungry and tired and depleted from all the sweating. I was ready to go back to civilization; yet, the return of the electrical power appeared to be imminent. On Monday morning, the electrical repair trucks were back, this time working to repair the damage they had looked at the day before. We were close to having power, but how close? By mid-morning there was still no power and I decided that enough was enough, and that I needed some of the creature comforts that civilization can provide—so I left.

By mid afternoon I arrived in Farmerville. My wife was miffed that I was gone so long but she understood after I explained about the faulty phone at our place. I told everyone that electrical power would soon be restored and that we would be returning home. Electricity was restored to our home the following Wednesday. On Friday, October 7, the Parish was allowing people to come back to Lake Charles. I spent the week at the Farmerville Library, vigorously pursuing any more forms of evacuee aid that might be out there for us, and also spending some time working on a paper about the Natalie Holloway case that I had been contemplating for some time. By Saturday morning, we were cleaning out our apartment, saying our heartfelt goodbyes to our hostess Pam Walker, and heading home.

October 9-October 22: These were possibly the two longest weeks of my life, with very little of any import going in with respect to when the school might reopen. The school president, Robert Hebert, had pledged that the semester would go on. About mid month, teaching fellows and adjunct professors received their paychecks on time; this was a hopeful sign. Meanwhile, the university's web site featured pictures of President Hebert and Provost Daboval working with state emergency management officials on plans to reopen the school. It appeared that school would start again, but when?

For much of the two weeks, there was little to report and anxiety was elevated for each day that there was no news. I had little trouble getting into my office although the school was officially still closed. Everyone's office door had been opened up for state officials to inspect the damage, file a report, and then fix any air quality problems. It turned out that this was what was holding up the reopening process.

As I walked across campus, the weather was brilliant: there had been almost no rain since the hurricane and temperatures were in the 70s with low humidity. I thought that the fall semester would have been spectacular, if only we'd had one. It appeared that whatever semester we had left would be a rushed one with long days and long hours being added to the class schedule to make up for all the classroom hours we'd missed. A campus cleanup day was thankfully cancelled when the Alabama National Guard graciously agreed to spend some of their time here cleaning up the campus. Still, a few pockets of debris lingered to remind us all of the storm.

Week of October 23: Word had leaked that this might be the week we get back to school once again, and I was greatly relieved. I lacked the nerve to ask about our October paychecks, as had other professors. We were all waiting on pins and pins and needles about that. In the meantime, we had applied for unemployment assistance.

On Tuesday, October 25 at a faculty meeting at Baker Hall on the McNeese campus, the professors and staff were told that school would resume Thursday, October 27 but that not all classes would begin at the same time. Classes would restart for the fall semester only if the building that you teach in had passed its air quality test. For those buildings that would not be reopening at all, temporary class buildings had been erected on the northern perimeter of the campus to accommodate displaced classes. My Thursday class of October 27th could not meet because the classroom had not passed its test yet. The same was true for my class on Friday, October 28th. However, I did communicate with both classes via Blackboard and urged patience.

Back to School

Week of October 30: By Monday, October 31st, all of my classrooms had been cleared, and the semester was underway after 5 weeks of delays related to

Hurricane Rita. I chose a cautious approach to teaching upon reentry; I trashed all the old syllabi and started from scratch. The initial class sessions were ones in which I negotiated a new syllabus with the students based upon student input and my own professional judgments. The second class sessions were a "syllabus day" in which the new syllabus was reviewed.

The campus scene was surreal. Only about half the students had returned. We were receiving reports of students who were kicked out of their apartments (due to storm damage to the apartments) and who were living in cars. Others had found refuge in a ship that was docked in the Port of Lake Charles. No luxury cruiser here: this was a ship that had been used to carry agricultural cargo around the world. The conditions were stark, but for many students this was a roof over their heads and they were glad to have it. The usual gaiety and laughter that accompanies student talk in the college quadrangle was missing. We went forward with Homecoming, but it was pared back, low-key and very subdued.

On campus, the building that housed the student cafeteria was not yet open, so a large white tent in the campus quadrangle served as the "mess tent" where meals were served. The massive white tent, a figurative elephant intruding in our midst, was a constant reminder of how much further the school had to go before things would have a sense of feeling normal. A portion of the Student Union that was a popular meeting place for students was also shut down, and the steps outside Farrar Hall became a new, impromptu place for students to hang out between classes.

As for myself, I could say that I was genuinely rested for one of the few times in recent years. The five weeks off had given me something that I could not have imagined, a chance to finally unwind and relax. I had not felt as good in years. It was like the fountain of youth. But how long would it last?

It was another matter for the students. They basically were looking at a "summer term" in order to finish up the fall semester, and summers are intense for everyone. But this was an incredible challenge for students—it was like a summer term where people were taking 18 hours of courses. During a conventional summer, 12 hours is considered a very heavy load, and students who attempt that tell me they will never do it again. Yet, that was the situation facing the students at McNeese, and they had little choice but to toughen up and get it over with. The graduating seniors were in the most distress; they had to toughen up and finish, or else they would not finish college on time as planned.

November 7-December 31: We got through this bizarre semester, and the faculty did all it could to accommodate the overwhelmed student body. In my classes, I made several adjustments to make the students' load and my own easier to carry. When the semester was over, I lacked the "dog tired" feeling I typically would have had, and I did not need the traditional 2 or 3 days in bed recovering from the whole affair. I was proud that the school honored its commitment to the university community to finish the semester against the long odds it faced in October, and I was especially proud of the Fall, 2005 graduates, which included a few New Orleans students, who would never forget their last semester of college. By the last week in December, the giant white mess tent was disassembled on the quadrangle, a symbol that things were getting back to normal.

Spring, 2006

There was still a long way to go before everything would be back to where it was before the storm. One dormitory never reopened. Several campus buildings are still closed at this point, with faculty and students displaced to offices and classrooms that are strange to them. The campus swimming pool and running track were closed with no word on when they would reopen, so my family had to make other arrangements for some of their recreational needs. In February, the library reopened to everyone's relief. The "Old Ranch" part of the Student Union also reopened, and the students regained one of their usual meeting places.

Some of the New Orleans students elected to stay at McNeese for at least one more semester before returning home, and we were glad to see these students once again. A few were missing and had not been heard from since their Rita evacuation. I was genuinely concerned about these students. FEMA had issued an order that Katrina evacuees who had secured motel rooms in Lake Charles were not to return to them, even to pick up any belongings left behind. This bureaucratic edict was cold and irrational, and a foregleam of the kinds of bureaucratic hell that people in New Orleans would eventually have to face.[17]

The spring semester began January 17, 2006 and the sense that I had of feeling well rested was starting to go away. I was feverishly working on some writing projects, as I knew that once the semester begins, teaching must take center stage at McNeese State, a Tier 4 teaching institution. By late February when the Mardi Gras break rolled around, I was literally hanging on waiting for it. The physical and emotional fatigue from the entire hurricane experience weighed on me now. My wife and I returned to Natchitoches, a charming Creole town in north Louisiana that we had discovered during our evacuation. We enjoyed the break but it was not nearly enough time off. On March 6, the second half of the semester was underway in earnest. Later in the month, I would go to the Southern Sociological Society to report on the New Orleans students that had been "doubly displaced" by Katrina and by Rita.[18]

Upon reflection, I must admit that I never used to think of myself as a privileged person. True, I am a white male and a college professor and have a lot of advantages to start with due the ascribed and achieved statuses that I hold. But teaching in the south, at a cash-starved Louisiana school mired in Tier 4 in the *U.S. News* rankings and feeling a bit underpaid for my efforts, I had never worn the mantle of privilege well. The hurricanes, Katrina and Rita, made me think differently about that.

I remember the horrid images of the people trapped at the Louisiana Superdome and at the New Orleans Convention Center. These are the people who were too poor to escape the storm. My family was fortunate enough to have two cars, about $100 in pocket money, and friends willing to help us out. The unfortunate individuals trapped in the sweltering heat of late summer New Orleans simply did not have the resources in either economic or social capital to get out of harm's way. Many of them are the ones who toil for minimum wage to make tourists to the city feel welcome. Now, they have been abandoned by government at all levels.

I was also very fortunate that once I was out of the way of the storm, I was in a position to pursue multiple forms of financial aid, and in the weeks afterward I was able to report that my family's meager bank account was in the best shape ever. I contrasted my own situation with the fate of many families in St. Bernard Parish, the Lower Ninth Ward, and south Mississippi that had lost everything and whose homes were cement slabs or piles of rubble with none of the most basic cleanup work even being started there. As I view the nightly pictures of these areas on CNN, I feel emotional pain for these families and I give thanks for having avoided catastrophe.

I looked forward to coming to New Orleans to the Southern Sociological Society to tell of my experiences. I was physically and emotionally drained, but I was excited about being in the French Quarter with some seldom seen colleagues and friends from graduate school. I appeared on a panel that was composed mostly of sociology faculty and graduate students from Tulane University. My first impression was that the pain of the diaspora was still very fresh.[19] Two of the first three speakers began to cry during their presentations. My own—in which I decided to relay the experiences of the 200 students from New Orleans that were doubly displaced by the two storms—ended early when I too became emotional and could not continue my comments. In addition to evacuee experiences, speakers on the panel spoke of the racism experienced by African Americans after the storm, the bureaucratic nightmares facing New Orleanians who returned to the city, and a close up look at the damage to one sociologist's home.[20] Chapter 4 of this book explains in more detail what this extraordinary session and conference was like.

In my diaspora experience I now have something in common in a minimal sort of way with diverse peoples much unlike me: sixth century B.C. Jews, famine and flood victims, refugees, Palestinians, people displaced by war and by hunger, the Acadians expulsed from Nova Scotia, and Katrina evacuees from New Orleans. As a privileged person I will never again take my social status for granted, and I pledge myself to use it as a tool to assist others in their hour of need.[21] For me personally, this is the most powerful legacy that remains from the two hurricanes.

Summer, 2006-Spring, 2007

A whirlwind of activity both personal and professional provided almost daily reminders of how much my life had become intertwined with the event. My niece married Steven Unkel, the Farmerville native and "lead driver" who led my family out of harm's way before the hurricane, on May 20, 2006 in Chattanooga, Tennessee. A reception for the couple was held in Lake Charles a week later.

During the break between the spring semester and the summer term, I toured Cameron Parish and Southeast Texas with Freddie Featherstone, the heroic brother in law who traveled from San Antonio to Lake Charles to inspect our home and report that it was mostly undamaged. Selected results of this tour appear as chapters in this book. Freddie moved to Lake Charles during 2006 along with his mother Ellen who had suffered the unexpected death of her husband, Fred Sr., in an industrial accident in Eastland, Texas.

During the summer, I polished up a few essays about the hurricane and decided to put them away for awhile in order to tend to other projects. Later in 2006, I revisited them and some of these essays appear in later chapters of this book.

My daughter visits Farmerville to see friends she made there, and my wife speaks to Pamela Walker on the phone occasionally. During 2006, Ms. Walker divorced her husband of over 30 years and she now lives in Nevada.

I kept in touch with the new friends I had made at the Southern Sociological Society in March, 2006. We decided to work on an article about our experiences and also a book length project, both of which are now thankfully completed and published.[22]

Summer, 2007-Spring, 2008

As the finishing touches to this chapter are being made, I struggle against the clock to complete it before the new hurricane season begins on June 1, 2008. Now, we relish every day during months when the season is out and dread every day when the season is in. In September, 2007 we received a one day scare from a very volatile stormed named Humberto. This unusual storm went from a tropical depression to a hurricane in just a few hours, and made landfall at Crystal Beach, Texas as a Category I hurricane. Frightfully close to the "boot" of southwestern Louisiana where Rita made landfall, it was a solemn reminder of just how volatile the Gulf of Mexico can be and how it should never be taken for granted. We can only hope and pray that the 2008 season, much like 2006 and most of 2007, will be mercifully absent of the kinds of destruction we saw in 2005.

NOTES

1. Danielle Antoinette Hidalgo, "After Hurricane Katrina: Storytelling Sociology." Paper presented at the annual meetings of the Southern Sociological Society, New Orleans, March, 2006.

2. For example, John Hill, "Baton Rouge: A City Under Stress." *Shreveport Times,* September 2, 2005.

3. Elliott R. Danzig, Paul W. Thayer and Lila R. Galanter, "The Effects of a Threatening Rumor on a Disaster Stricken Community." Washington, D.C.: National Academy of Sciences, National Research Council, 1958.

4. Erving Goffman, *The Presentation of Self in Everyday Life*. Garden City, NY: Doubleday, 1959.

5. Lianne Hart, David Zucchino and James Rainey, "A City in Survival Mode Restoring Order." *Los Angeles Times*, September 4, 2005.

6. Solomon Asch, *A Study of Change in Mental Organization*. New York: Archives of Psychology, 1936; Stanley Milgram, *Obedience to Authority*. New York: HarperPerrenial, 1974.

7. Doug McAdam and Gary T. Marx, *Collective Behavior and Social Movements*. Englewood Cliffs, N.J.: Prentice Hall, 1994.

8. The "look and leave" program allows residents to temporarily inspect the damage to their homes during the day, and then they must leave during the night time hours when the police cannot guarantee the homeowners' safety. This is a temporary program available for the convenience of residents before public officials issue an "all clear" message that it is safe for everyone to return.

9. Katherine Mangan, "Colleges Hit by Rita Face Major Repairs and an Uncertain Future." *Chronicle of Higher Education*, October 7, 2005.

10. Robert Merton, "Social Structure and Anomie." *American Sociological Review*, 3, 1938, pp. 672-682.

11. Michel Foucault, *Discipline and Punish: The Birth of the Prison*. New York: Pantheon Books, 1977.

12. Jennifer Day, "Harassment on the Streets." Paper presented at the annual meetings of the Southern Sociological Society, New Orleans, March, 2006.

13. For example, Stephanie Scurlock, "Hurricane Sex Offenders Living in Midsouth Neighborhoods." *News 3*, Memphis, Tennessee, March 31, 2006.

14. Erving Goffman, *Frame Analysis*. New York: Harper and Row, 1974.

15. Earl Babbie, *Adventures in Social Research*. Thousand Oaks, CA: Pine Forge Press, 1995.

16. Seymour Fisher, "Personal Interview." University of Texas Medical Branch, Galveston, TX, December 15, 1993.

17. Tim Haney, "Bureaucratic Issues and Hurricane Katrina." Paper presented at the annual meetings of the Southern Sociological Society, New Orleans, March, 2006.

18. See Jessica Pardee, "Disaster Experiences of Low Income Families Facing Hurricane Katrina." Paper presented at the annual meetings of the Southern Sociological Society, New Orleans, March.

19. Hidalgo, ibid.

20. Danielle Hidalgo, Kristen Barber, Jessica Pardee, Andrea Wilbon, Tim Haney, Jennifer Day, April Brayfield (and myself) presented papers at this session that was entitled, "Ongoing Stories, Ongoing Struggles."

21. Alvin Gouldner, *The Coming Crisis of Western Sociology*. New York: Basic Books, 1970; C. Wright Mills, *The Sociological Imagination*. New York: Oxford University Press, 1959; Dan Clawson (Ed.), *Public Sociology*. Berkeley, CA: University of California Press, 2007.

22. Kristen Barber, Danielle Antoinette Hidalgo, Timothy Haney, Stan Weeber, Jessica Pardee, and Jennifer Day. "Narrating the Storm: Storytelling as a Methodological

Approach to Understanding Hurricane Katrina." *Journal of Public Management and Social Policy,* 13, (2), 2007, pp. 99-120; Danielle Antoinette Hidalgo and Kristen Barber (Eds.), *Narrating the Storm: Sociological Stories of Hurricane Katrina.* Newcastle: Cambridge Scholars Press, 2007.

Chapter 2

Remembering McNeese State

At McNeese State, classes began on a staggered basis on October 27, 2005, 37 days after the campus evacuated ahead of Hurricane Rita. The road to recovery was full of bureaucratic roadblocks few could have anticipated. As soon as power was restored to the campus and local officials gave the "all clear" signal for evacuated residents to return, work began to restore the campus. The President and Provost initiated an intense collaborative effort between local, parish, state and federal officials to reopen the school as soon as humanly possible. Yet, there was a long delay that proved frustrating to all in the university community.

A major contributing factor was the slow pace of infrastructure repair due to resources being tied up in the New Orleans recovery following Katrina. In particular, in Lake Charles there was a lack of state inspectors that must, by state law, certify that a building can be reentered safely. A building occupied by Louisiana state employees must be re-inspected and recertified as habitable by such inspectors if the building was shut down unexpectedly for three days or more. Inspection personnel were already spread thin, dealing with the heavy burden of inspecting state owned or leased buildings closed due to Katrina. Among the last of these inspection hurdles for any given building was the air quality test to certify that the building's air is free of asbestos and other toxins.

As I waited patiently for school to restart, I was having some difficult thoughts about my occupational life and my work. My personal life including that of my family had gone well after the storm, but as I left home to go in to work, I harbored dark thoughts about the road ahead. I was not sure that I was cut out for the tasks that would be on my calendar shortly. By the third week of October, I felt I like I had reached a very low point mentally with respect to my work. As I sat at my desk during this hiatus, the long delay in starting school only proved to me that I am basically powerless to influence much of the really important events in my life. I was totally dependent upon state officials in Baton Rouge, upon state building inspectors, and upon my university administration. Even during my evacuation, I had felt that I was powerless to do anything to improve my fate. I had to wait 16 days for forces more powerful than myself to get things done—mainly public officials in Lake Charles and electrical workers from out of state—so that I could return home. Then, there was the issue of how to proceed in my classes, which was the main sticking point and greatest issue of concern.

My insecurities focused on the idea that I was no longer an authority on how best to teach my classes. I could not recall a graduate level class that had anything to do with how to teach sociology after a hurricane. Where is the script? I felt like the director of a play for which there was no script and not even any ideas for a basic plot that would allow the production to proceed. And the start of school was bearing down; it was only a few days away.

Stephen Brookfield's work on "critically reflective teaching" was thrust toward the front of my consciousness during this personal low point, giving me a much needed sense of direction.[1] For Brookfield, skillful teaching is tied to student outcomes, particularly the student's own sense that something has been learned along with the student's acquisition of a world view that contains a critical lens. Such teaching is not the storybook version of teaching or grounded in the teacher's sense of how teaching ought to be. Instead, it is one in which mutual respect, negotiation, collaborativeness and praxis are present for both teacher and learner.[2] The process by which this occurs is a creative, unscripted, messy pursuit—he called it "the educational equivalent of white water rafting"[3] I could understand this fully: the rapids were straight ahead and I had no plan.

Fundamental to skillful teaching is the art of "critically reflective teaching," teaching that is guided by a critical rationale but adapts to students' experience of learning and to the contextual variables of classroom life. In critically reflective teaching, you become aware of how students experience learning. This might mean a painful process of reframing purposes, methods, and evaluative criteria in your teaching, as the dominant themes or concerns emerge from your students. Though the changes might be painful, such teaching and learning may be liberating to both professor and student, as each peels away ideological assumptions that may have previously restricted the way they approach the context of the classroom setting.[4] Brookfield believed that there were four aspects to critical reflection: (1) obtaining the students' view; (2) obtaining our colleagues' perceptions; (3) reading the theoretical literature guiding our work; and (4) studying the details of our own autobiographies.[5]

It occurred to me that my colleagues and I had already heeded at least part of Brookfield's advice without taking note of it. We had agreed, with our boss's urging, to be charitable to students after Katrina and to obtain the student's view of their own situations at that time. This would continue after Rita. Speaking for myself and perhaps some colleagues, I had contemplated the pedagogical writings of sociology and found them deficient in the situation after Rita. And, I had obviously already pondered the insecure low points of my own post Rita biography. Now, we needed to carry on what we had started after Katrina, this time factoring in our Rita experience and letting Brookfield be our guide.

Brookfield provided even more assistance to me by suggesting that the most significant learning we undergo as adults results from some external event or stimulus that causes us to engage in an anxiety producing and uncomfortable reassessment of aspects of our personal, occupational, and relational lives. Such "critical incidents" are vivid learning experiences as they stand out in sharp relief from the canvas of more mundane experiences, and highlight the ways in which students really learn things.[6] For me, my colleagues and my students such a critical event was the experience of evacuating and/or readjusting following the two hurricanes. Separated from the familiar comforts of home with little money and leaning on the generosity of others, the evacuation experience in particular is rife with uncertainty and the bleak realization that there may be nothing left of your former lives. This is certainly "hitting bottom," a profoundly "critical incident" that could inform both teaching and learning upon our return to school.

After the long delay, all of my classrooms passed inspection by late October, and my classes were finally underway on October 31. If Brookfield was to be my guide, I had to continue to do the right things; I had to follow his lead. I sent out a memo before the first class period via Blackboard to let students know that classes would be resuming. Humbled greatly by the storm and emboldened by Brookfield, a new sense of democracy took hold of me. I approached the first class as a "class meeting" whereby a new set of class requirements could be negotiated by the students and instructor. This was a new start, a new exercise in mutual respect and colalborativeness. After five weeks of no school, the requirements and the timetable for classroom requirements set forth in the original syllabus were now obsolete.

I was teaching two sections of Introductory Sociology and two sections of advanced sociology. When I asked introductory students how many tests they wanted, they surprisingly said that they wanted 4 tests including the final, which was the requirement on the original syllabus that they received in August. They thought that the more opportunities to be tested, the greater the chances of success in the class. They had taken their first test on Wednesday, September 21, the day before Lake Charles evacuated ahead of Rita. I therefore scheduled 3 more tests, with a non-comprehensive final test during a revised finals week that was scheduled for the week of December 18th. However, the four original homework assignments were reduced to two; these being assignments that required reading and processing information on the Internet and formulating answers to some critical thinking questions. The two assignments cut were library assignments requiring library research. Frazer Memorial Library was still closed due to the storm and would not reopen until February, 2006. I also waived the attendance policy that was created in 2003 to encourage student attendance. After Rita, I saw no way that the policy could be enforced. Class periods were lengthened (by the administration) to make up for the contact hours lost due to the storm. Class discussion of critical concepts such as bureaucracy and the power elite were enlivened by stories of official racism, sexism and indifference after the hurricane.

In the advanced classes, the atmosphere was much different. Perhaps due to the predominance of older and some non traditional students who were carrying heavy work and child care responsibilities, students were begging for leniency and mercy. My Sociological Theory class had already taken test 1, or at least the hearty souls who had not yet fled the oncoming storm as of September 20— about one half of the class. This meant that half the class was caught up and the other half wasn't. Given the circumstances, I decided to have a staggered start to the class: those who had taken test 1 were allowed the week off to tend to other responsibilities while those who had not taken the test were given the opportunity to "re-review" for the test and to take it. The assignments were reduced from four to two. The number of tests was reduced from 4 to 3, with the final non-comprehensive test being a "take home" test. As long as I've taught, I had vowed never to allow take home tests, but I changed my mind with the urging of students in this particular situation. The term paper requirement for the class was cancelled as the library was closed. The attendance requirement was waived, as was the case in the introductory classes. A conflict paradigm grounded in Marx, Dahrendorf, and the Frankfurt theorists was given more attention than usual given the lack of bureaucratic and media response to the aftermath of Rita.

The second advanced class, ironically, was Collective Behavior and Social Movements, which had some lecture segments on the sociology of disaster. Needless to say, there was much of current interest to discuss, much of it counter-intuitive to what the research literature had argued with respect to the "functionality" of behavior post-disaster.[7] A new post-Katrina research agenda in the sociology of disaster was noted, including differential race/class/gender outcomes during the evacuation and readjustment process.

About a week before school started in late October, I received a memo from the Director of Electronic Learning asking me to convert this Collective Behavior class, which was a Wednesday night class meeting from 5:25 to 8:05 P.M. into a distance learning class as the originally assigned classroom in the Burton Business Center had not yet passed the air quality test and might not do so for some time to come. I agreed, as the class was set up on Blackboard to perform just about all classroom functions except for testing. Just as school was about to begin, I received another memo indicating that a classroom had now been located and that the class no longer needed to be distance learning. I now had a decision to make: distance learning or not? I asked the Director what to do and her answer was an intriguing one: "why not let the students decide what direction the class will take?"[8] I decided to take her advice, as I believe Brookfield would have.

At the first available class meeting on Wednesday night, November 2, I arranged for a "class meeting" in the designated classroom. I sent an email via Blackboard indicating that this will be a class meeting in which the format for the remainder of the class would be decided. About half the class attended, with many others who could not attend weighing in via email.

There were many graduating seniors in this class. For them, it was a particularly stressful time. Some had already lined up jobs and were simply completing their academic credentials. These students in particular faced a situation that was most stressful: in order to graduate on time and enter the workforce on time, they had to stand tall and complete whatever requirements their professors gave them in the extraordinary circumstances they found themselves in. Some were living in shelters, or in ships docked at the Port of Lake Charles; others in cramped FEMA trailers. They had to balance school with work and family responsibilities in many cases. Given these manifold hurdles I decided to show leniency and mercy. The class voted for and received an online class. I scheduled only two take home tests, one over material that had already been covered before the hurricane (the last activity before the storm had been a review for the first test), and one non comprehensive take home test at the very end of the semester and due during the revised finals week. As in the other advanced classes, the two critical thinking assignments were assigned and the term paper requirement was eliminated. Take home test 1 was due November 16th; and take home test 2 was due December 19th. The two assignments were also due December 19th.

Conclusion

The most bizarre semester in McNeese history ended on December 23, 2005 when 752 students, including scores of social science majors and a few displaced seniors from New Orleans, graduated from the school after an accelerated eight weeks of intensive study. Though the semester was over, my critical thinking about my own situation was definitely incomplete.

The utter powerlessness I felt as I waited for school to resume was not something unique to me. Several other faculty, in sociology and other disciplines, felt the need for greater advocacy and input regarding decisions that affect their academic lives and futures. My supervisor, for example, served on a committee that issued an after-action report on the university's response to the hurricanes. One key recommendation was that state law be amended to waive some of the strict requirements regarding infrastructure repair, allowing local contractors to work in good faith to repair the campus in the shortest amount of time possible. For my part, I accepted an invitation to speak at the Southern Sociological Society on a panel about how local sociologists coped with the storms and their aftermaths (see Chapter 4). The panel, mostly Tulane University graduate students and faculty, was well received. Several in the audience suggested that we compile our sociological stories in book form. Under the direction of two panelists we did that, and also contributed a paper to a journal on public management and social policy. Key issues that we identified and discussed in the paper: the emotional attachment to place as well as the blasé attitude among residents that prevents evacuation; the inadequacies of bureaucracies in meeting our basic needs; and the masculinization of space in disaster recovery zones.[9]

At another level, I broke free from a number of inhibitions that I'd had regarding online learning and accelerated learning. Like many faculty, I had accumulated years of ideological baggage that caused me to discriminate against this kind of pedagogy. Students needed a certain amount of time to learn and reflect, and this must necessarily require a 16 week "lecture and test" experience. The post-hurricane experience opened my eyes to new avenues of teaching and learning. Utilizing the flexibility exercised after the hurricane, by the fall of 2008 I was teaching Introductory Sociology online, and both advanced classes taught during the fall of 2005 were now 8 week online accelerated classes.

NOTES

1. Stephen Brookfield, *The Skillful Teacher*. San Francisco: Jossey-Bass, 2006; *The Power of Critical Theory*. San Francisco: Jossey-Bass, 2005; *Becoming a Critically Reflective Teacher*. San Francisco: Jossey-Bass, 1995; *The Skillful Teacher*. San Francisco: Jossey-Bass, 1990; *Understanding and Facilitating Adult Learning*. San Francisco: Jossey-Bass, 1986.

2. Brookfield, 1995.

3. Brookfield, 1990, p. 2.

4. Brookfield, 2005.

5. Brookfield, 1995.

6. Brookfield, 1990.

7. See Charles Fritz and J.H. Mathewson, *Convergence Behavior in Disasters; A Problem of Social Control*. Washington, D.C.: National Research Council, 1957; Charles Fogleman, *Family and Community in Disaster: A Socio-Psychological Study of the Effects of a Major Disaster Upon Individuals and Groups Within the Impact Area*. Ph.D. Dissertation, Louisiana State University, 1958; Russell Dynes, *Organized Behavior in Disaster*. Lexington, MA: Heath Lexington Books, 1970; Frederick L. Bates, *The Social and Psychological Consequences of a Natural Disaster: A Longitudinal Study of Hurricane Audrey*. Washington, D.C.: National Academy of Sciences, National Research Council, 1963; Kai Erickson, *A New Species of Trouble: Explorations in Disaster, Trauma, and Community*. New York: W. W. Norton and Company, 1994; Henry Fischer, *Response to Disaster: Fact Versus Fiction and its Perpetuation: The Sociology of Disaster*. Lanham, MD: University Press of America, 1998; Harry Moore, *Before the Wind: A Study of the Response to Hurricane Carla*. Washington, D.C.: National Research Council, 1963; *Tornadoes Over Texas; A Study of Waco and San Angelo in Disaster*. Austin, TX: University of Texas Press, 1958; George Baker, *Man and Society in Disaster*. New York: Basic Books, 1962; Allen Barton, *Communities in Disaster; A Sociological Analy-

sis of Collective Stress Situations. New York: Doubleday, 1969; Kenneth Wilkinson and Peggy Ross, *Citizens' Responses to Warnings of Hurricane Camille*. State College, MS: Social Science Research Center, Mississippi State University, 1970; Michael Dyson, *Come Hell or High Water: Hurricane Katrina and the Color of Disaster*. New York: Basic Civitas, 2006; Brayfield, *ibid*; Haney, *ibid*; Hidalgo, *ibid*.

8. Thanks to Dr. Helen Ware, Director of Electronic Learning at McNeese State for this most helpful suggestion.

9. Hidalgo and Barber, *ibid*.

Chapter 3

Remembering the New Orleanians

This chapter is the narrative story of the 224 New Orleans college students who relocated to Lake Charles, Louisiana following Hurricane Katrina, and then only days later, were forced to evacuate again due to Hurricane Rita. I do not know the personal stories of all 224 students, but I knew enough of the stories so that a sociological narrative could be constructed that recognizes varieties of experiences. Because I am a sociologist and the students that I knew were sociology students, the story is punctuated with sociological musings. The writings of sociological micro theorists such as Erving Goffman were remembered as I retraced the students' long and worrisome experience of living through the two storms. It is possible that the New Orleanians' double diaspora is something unique or at least very rare in the annals of American academe.

This is a story of immense emotional pain, suffering, coping, readjustment, and redemption. The pains are writ so large upon the soul that mere words cannot describe them, nor can sociological musings and observations make the pain more manageable. The pains are etched into the psyche by repetition, by the double horror experienced by these students.

As mentioned in the opening narrative in Chapter 1, the effects of Katrina felt in Lake Charles were more social than physical. As the storm blew through south Louisiana in late August Lake Charles experienced only a brief afternoon shower. By the next day, social waves from the storm were felt here. After a special needs shelter had been constructed on the McNeese campus and our Burton Coliseum opened to evacuees, we began to see the first of the New Orleanians who came to McNeese to study on an emergency basis. The social science faculty did all it could to accommodate these new students, being encouraged to do so in an August 30 memo from our head, Billy Turner.[1]

As we've already seen in Chapter 1, natural disasters and their aftermaths tend to be breeding grounds for rumor. After Katrina rumors quickly spread that Katrina evacuees in Baton Rouge, Lake Charles, and other towns were hijacking cars, robbing businesses, raping women, and fomenting riots. These rumors were mostly untrue but caused a wave of fear among the locals. The rumors marginalized the 200 plus evacuee students at McNeese even though very few if any of the townsfolk in Lake Charles actually thought the students culpable in any way of the of the purported crimes. The mere fact that the crimes were supposedly being committed by "outsiders" meant that a deviant status, completely unearned, was being unexpectedly thrust upon the students, who were themselves outsiders by definition.[2] Though the school tried hard to accommodate the students, the use of the term "refugee" to refer to them did connote some underlying sense that the students were being marginalized, even within the academy. On September 4, Billy Turner issued another memo asking faculty to refrain from calling students "refugees" as some had taken offense to this demeaning term that suggested a lack of respect for the new students.[3]

Cheryse, a 22 year old single parent and freshman from New Orleans, arrived on the McNeese campus at an importune time. The shock of her diaspora wore on her distraught face as she wandered from building to unknown building, hoping to find where she could restart her education. Almost by chance, she wandered upon the Registrar's Office in Kaufman Hall where she was able to fill out her student paperwork and enroll in classes.

Her angst intensified many times as she tried to locate her first class. She found the building and the classroom, but at the appointed hour, 8 A.M., there were no students and no professor in the class. She then went to find help—to the Dean's Office of the College of Business, to the Registrar's Office, to the Department Head of Social Science, and finally to the instructor. It turned out that the class had been cancelled for the week, with students being asked to help out in Katrina relief efforts while the professor (actually, me) attended to some committee work that had been assigned to him during the 8 o'clock hour by mistake. Cheryse felt somewhat better as she met with me and found out that by using the classroom software Blackboard, she would be able to access class lecture notes, assignments, and most of the information she needed to catch up. At the end of her conference with me, she turned and left suddenly, without thanking me for my efforts, and still feeling a deep sense of betrayal by the McNeese system.

Chandra, a 20 year old freshman from New Orleans, was just settling into a new life in Lake Charles, and was making good progress judging from her conversation with me on September 14 following my Wednesday evening lecture on Collective Behavior and Social Movements. Though still in shock over her situation, she was becoming more grounded in it. She told me that when she left New Orleans, she was expecting to be gone for just a few days. There had been an evacuation during Hurricane Ivan in 2004, and as the hurricane missed New Orleans, people returned after a short while. She was hoping that that would be the case with Katrina. Now more settled in the reality of her situation, she was trying to accentuate the positive by discussing some of the more laudatory aspects of Lake Charles, such as the low price of housing here. And now, she was looking forward to forming a school routine by studying collective behavior and other subjects. Because the study of collective behavior involves the sociological study of disasters, I wove as many references to Katrina as I could into the lecture of September 14th, and Chandra appeared to enjoy that. She appeared to be connecting the subject matter to her own diaspora.

Students who entered school after Cheryse and Chandra appeared to be have encountered some dire circumstances. A student in the hallway near the Registrar's Office still managed to smile at me despite the bright red color of her face, which suggested that she had been out in the hot miserable weather of New Orleans, possibly on a rooftop with no shade, waiting to be rescued for several days. Further down the hall, student athletes from New Orleans colleges filled out the requisite NCAA paperwork that would allow them to temporarily transfer to McNeese State to continue their educations. Shocked silence was the order of the day, interrupted only by questions whispered to each other or to the athletic compliance officer who coordinated the students' entry to MSU. Several of these students entered an independent study class that I taught, Sociology 451Q.

A coping strategy of some of the less confrontational New Orleanians was simply to "blend in" with the regularly enrolled McNeese students or try to "pass" as one of them.[4] Late registration had been extended, and a good many McNeese students were taking advantage of the unscheduled extension to "shop" for easier professors and classes. Blending into the crowd was the easy choice for some of the newcomers. They accomplished this by not making any notation or any other signification at all to me about being students from New Orleans. The evacuated students were indicated by a special code in the McNeese record keeping system that designated them as undecided majors. If I was not aware of their status (and I was often too busy to pay attention to the special code), the student could just quietly blend in with the already registered McNeese students, hoping to slip in as late entrants. These students were taking advantage of a long history of a socially embedded conversation[5] that goes on between faculty and students during late registration that goes something like this: "Hi, I'm Joe Smith and I'm enrolling late in your class ... what do I have to do to catch up?" With growing pressure for higher enrollments, these late entrants appear more often than ever, even after the late registration period has expired. So having "late, late" enrollees is not all that rare anymore. Several of the New Orleans students I got to know—Michelle, Lindsay, Renee, Melinda, and Robin (pseudonyms)—used this figurative conversation as a cover to slip into classes unnoticed as Katrina evacuees. Perhaps painfully aware of how New Orleanians were being typecast outside the university, these students did not want to suffer guilt by association if they were to reveal their evacuee status. For these quiet and unobtrusive entrants (at least in their approach to me) I discovered their evacuee status well after the fact. By not highlighting it and by not even raising their status during my earliest discussions with them, they chose to forego all the advantages that could have been reaped from making their statuses known. I believe that they feared a backlash if they had done so, although other factors could have come into play to explain their behavior.

In contrast, another line of behavior I noted as the New Orleanians approached their new school was to approach the instructor as an evacuee and to humbly ask how they could "catch up" to the material that the other students had already studied. By deploying their "evacuee self," the students were hoping to save "face;" that is, they aimed to achieve a positive presentation of self.[6] They hoped that freely admitting their evacuee status would portend some generosity or leniency on the part of the instructor, and that any shortfalls in student performance might be tactfully ignored or "disattended" due to their unique circumstances.[7] Alex (pseudonym), a 32-year-old senior, stood out as an exemplar of this approach. After his first appearance at my Sociological Theory class, he warmly greeted me, identifying himself as a new student from New Orleans. I enthusiastically greeted him back, welcoming him to class and letting him know that I was here to help him during the semester. This approach worked well for both of us. His easy-going, humble, and willing attitude in self-presentation reflected an effort to gain as much "face" as possible and to "establish himself," or to establish "footing," on the professor's good side. I reciprocated by letting Alex know how to access the class lecture notes on Blackboard and catch up on the assigned readings.

Hurricane Rita

As mentioned in the initial narrative, Tropical Storm Rita became the 17th named storm of the 2005 season on Sunday, September 18. This news produced no particular concerns in southwest Louisiana, which had not seen a major storm since Audrey in 1957. Early models had Rita delivering a glancing blow to the Florida Keys and then after that, a westward plunge into the Gulf of Mexico.

On Wednesday, September 21 at 8 AM I finished handing out a test to a section of students in Introductory Sociology. Despite the hurricane now looming close to Louisiana in the Gulf, attendance was good—even the New Orleans students were attending. As I looked vacantly at the students from my perch in the front, the question that weighed heaviest on my mind was not about who was cheating on the test or who wasn't, but this: where will my family be this weekend? For the New Orleans students, this thought was "off the charts" so to speak; some had been separated from family members and were still reeling with the heart wrenching question left over from Katrina, "where is my family?"

When I had opportunities to speak with the New Orleans students, they were seriously restless and frightened by Rita. A sizeable portion of their city was still under water and the broken levees were patched up but not yet repaired. Flood water was being pumped out but the process was very slow. Being hit by Rita would mean more water cascading over the broken levees, and a double dose of misery for the Crescent City. There was talk of a second evacuation of New Orleans. The displaced students wondered if this second catastrophe might permanently disable their city and might discourage efforts to rebuild it.[8]

My Wednesday night class had to go on at 5:25 P.M. even though the school would be shut down for the next two days. Several in the class wondered why the Wednesday night classes were meeting as stores were already running out of supplies and the time spent in class would only delay the students' efforts to assist their families. I can't say that I blamed them for thinking that. As I mentioned in the first chapter, I had forgotten my notes for that evening's test review, so I was having to work harder than I thought I should have. My mind raced as I tried to concentrate on the review and also to look for Chandra and Michelle who entered the class last week after leaving New Orleans. Taking no chances at all, they had already fled ahead of Rita.

Evacuation

Anyone who got up early the next day, September 22nd, could see that southwestern Louisiana was in some danger and that if the storm turned even more northward, there would be severe consequences for Cameron and Calcasieu Parishes, the two parishes closest to the Gulf in this part of the state. By 8 A.M., the mandatory evacuation was issued for everyone in the parish south of Interstate 10. For the New Orleans students, this was a horror more vivid than anything that they could make up or experience during their worst dreams. The more frightened ones left early, others left only when ordered to go, awakened from early morning sleep with the bad news. No one that I knew of defied the evacuation order and stayed behind. After making some phone calls later, I learned that some of the students had fled to Arkansas. I prayed for Godspeed in sending them to a safe place. They could not go home, as there was some risk that Rita would still have an impact in New Orleans with renewed flooding. The students also wondered what would be the result of this evacuation. Are they leaving for a few days as they had thought before (before Katrina's landfall); or was this the beginning of another long period of readjustment and agonizing pain in a new and unknown place?

By 10 P.M. that evening, my family had arrived by car at its destination, Farmerville, Louisiana. A stark, unfurnished two bedroom apartment had been offered us and we gratefully accepted. My family had only been able to scrape together $100 in pocket money and to fill up our two cars with gas. We were fortunate indeed to have friends who took care of us. I thought for a moment about the very unfortunate New Orleans students. They had been uprooted once and perhaps separated from family; now it was happening again—some being shipped off to who knows where on a bus with a group of strangers. In Farmerville, I ran into a former student of mine who was living in Sulphur, Louisiana and who was a native of a town close to Farmerville called Bernice. Maybe it is a "small world" as Stanley Milgram had once suggested.[9] As for the New Orleans students, I could only hope that at some point in their reevacuation they had been fortunate enough to reconnect with someone that they knew from back home. It was their only chance of finding something familiar in this unbelievably strange "new normal."

On Friday, September 23rd I found myself in uncharted territory. There is no more helpless feeling for an addicted "news hound" than to be shut out of the news, but that was my plight this morning. There was no news of the storm anywhere. I figured if I was in the dark, then the New Orleans students must have been similarly frustrated. It is indeed possible that some of these students who took buses out of Lake Charles may not have had any real sense of where they were going and probably lacked any familiarity at all with the places that they were being bused to. Then, there were painful thoughts about family members from whom they had been separated, and how it would become even more difficult for them to be reunited after life had been turned upside down a second time. To make matters worse, any personal belongings that they left behind in Lake Charles could be swept away in a strong storm surge from Rita, and that was exactly what was being predicted as I looked at the Internet on this painful Friday night at Pam Walker's house. I wondered how many of the New Orleanians had access to that information at that moment; my gut suspicion was that few if any did.

The next day, my family felt blessed as we discovered the news that Rita hit Sabine Pass, Texas as a Category 2 storm. Lake Charles was near the fierce northeast eye wall of the storm but did not receive a Katrina like punch. There was no major flooding. And we had found out early in the afternoon that our home had survived the storm with only minor damage. This was the exact news that every evacuee wants to know from the moment that the storm has passed through his or her town, and we got the news quickly. I thought about the displaced New Orleans students who would still have to wait another month or more to find out what happened to their homes, and who would likely face some long delays before finding out how their temporary homes in Lake Charles had fared.

Back to School

During the very long three weeks that we waited for building inspectors to inspect our classrooms and offices, I had my first "re-encounters" with the New Orleanians. They latched on to me (figuratively if not literally) as someone familiar in the landscape of woes they had endured as double evacuees. They were indeed glad to see me and to reestablish our relationship, although in reality I was someone they barely knew. Still, I was a connection to Lake Charles and to something that was stable and predictable within the sea of chaos they had experienced—an academic routine. And strategically, I was an important piece of the puzzle as they contemplated getting through this nightmare semester with a set of grades and some feeling that progress was being made on their degrees. For a few of the students, this was their final undergraduate semester—one they would surely never forget, and they were very concerned as most graduating seniors are with their making sure that they have completed all of the course requirements. So it was with these seniors that I had the most contact after I arrived back in Lake Charles.

Alex, the 32 year old senior that hoped to make the most of his final semester by unabashedly engaging his evacuee self, was grateful to be graduating but also mourning an experience that had died with the two hurricanes. This semester he was scheduled to take a Political Philosophy class that he had looked forward to taking for some time under one of his favorite professors at Tulane. It was this class in particular above all others that he was eagerly looking forward to. He relished the idea of going to class, taking notes, taking the tests and working on the term paper. I wondered if the Sociological Theory class Alex was taking with me at McNeese with me had been equally satisfying; I suspect not. And certainly that was one of the aspects of Tulane that he missed—a Tier 1 school with an excellent faculty and the ability of that faculty to teach some specialty classes that they had great interest in. Thus, his graduation was bittersweet. I asked him if he would go back to Tulane to audit a few classes he'd missed. He said (with apparent honesty) no, that it was time to move on with his life and that he had suffered enough.

Cheryse reconnected with me and was glad to be back in school. She was friendlier now and my original harsh assessment of her had softened—in fact I had completely forgiven her for her childish first day tantrum. As a single parent, she bore the pressure of providing for her family under these most difficult circumstances. The 8 o'clock class that she was taking with me (originally a class from 8 to 8:50 AM) had been changed to a 65 minute course from 7:30-8:35 A.M. This was so that the class would have enough contact hours in order to finish the semester. I was teaching another section of the course at 4:30 in the afternoon and she asked if she could attend the afternoon class as she was having trouble arranging for child care and then showing up at class on time at 7:30. I consented to this request, considering the pain that she had been through. Eventually she successfully completed the class, and was she elated to have finished the fall semester.

We somehow managed to survive the strange semester, and the faculty did all it could within reason to accommodate people like Cheryse and the entire overwhelmed student body. In my classes (see Chapter 2), I cut the number of homework assignments in half, reduced the number of tests, and cancelled term papers as the library had not yet reopened. I allowed students to do a "take home" final, something I thought myself too old fashioned ever to allow. The students were laboring hard but I was rested and was enjoying myself. I was proud that the school honored its commitment to the university community to finish the semester considering the long odds it had faced in October. On graduation night in late December, a few of the New Orleanians graduated from their home colleges but "walked the stage" with their new friends from McNeese State.

Endgame

The displaced students underwent a series of changes as they lived through this nightmarish though historic semester. They learned more about themselves, especially how tough and adaptable they were. They felt that if they could withstand two hurricanes and two evacuations, they could survive most anything. They vowed never to take their educations for granted. For those returning home, there was a vow to appreciate all the advantages, cultural and otherwise, of going to school and living in the great city of New Orleans. Cheryse probably spoke for many when she exclaimed: "Good old New Orleans! My people are there, my school's there, my heart is there. Time to go. That's where I belong."[10]

NOTES

1. Billy Turner, memo to the Social Science Faculty of McNeese State University, August 30, 2005.

2. Howard Becker, *Outsiders*. London: Free Press of Glencoe, 1963.

3. Billy Turner, memo to the Social Science Faculty of McNeese State University, September 4, 2005.

4. Erving Goffman, *Stigma*. Englewood Cliffs, N.J.: Prentice Hall, 1963.

5. Erving Goffman, *Forms of Talk*. Philadelphia: University of Pennsylvania Press, 1981.

6. Erving Goffman, *Interaction Ritual*. Garden City, NY: Anchor Books, 1967.

7. Goffman, 1959, 1974.

8. Charles Babington, "Hastert Tries Damage Control After Remarks Hit a Nerve." *Washington Post*, September 3, 2005, p. A17.

9. Ithiel De Sola Pool, Stanley Milgram, Theodore Newcomb and Manfred Kochen, *The Small World*. Norwood, N.J.: Ablex Publishers, 1989.

10. Author's final meeting with Cheryse, May, 2006.

Chapter 4

Remembering the 2006 SSS Meetings

On the way to the Big Easy, I didn't know what to expect. Would it really be "the city with no people?" Others told me crime and violence were rampant, in fact much worse than they used to be. "Watch out at night! The criminal underbelly exposes itself then."[1] A few whispered that my every move would be monitored, because so few are present: the panopticon effect.[2] I wondered, too, about how the people who came back had coped with the distress of their diaspora. Within a few hours, I would start to find out.

As a sociologist, my days are filled teaching students and studying human groups and their problems and prospects. Today, I was going to do something unconventional: tell the story of the 224 college students from New Orleans who escaped Hurricane Katrina by evacuating to Lake Charles, only to be forced to evacuate a second time during Hurricane Rita. Their double evacuation was very unique if not unprecedented in the history of American academe.

I was the only speaker not from Tulane or from New Orleans on this March, 2006 panel at the annual meetings of the Southern Sociological Society, and the only one not to be directly affected by Katrina. The panel, excepting myself, consisted of sociologists and graduate students in sociology from Tulane University. The title of the panel was "Ongoing Stories, Ongoing Struggles" and was designed so that conventioneers from out of town could attend this panel and get the "locals" view of Hurricane Katrina. "Sociological storytelling" was the format for the presentations.[3] I was amazed at how warmly I was received by the people from Tulane, and how they seated me in the middle of the panelists. Although I was the only speaker who had experienced Rita, I was not being marginalized at this conference.

At the time of the SSS annual meetings, it had been seven months since Katrina hit, but I can tell you in no uncertain terms that the pain of the diaspora was very fresh for everyone on the panel. You could see it in their voices or in their faces, or in both. The mood at the outset, and indeed throughout the panel's 75 minutes of allotted time, was subdued, even mournful.

Danielle Hidalgo was the first speaker and the one who had done the most work in organizing this panel on sociological storytelling after Katrina. Early in her presentation she began to cry as she related her story of watching the horrid images of the hurricane on TV and wondering, from her home in California, what had become of her Tulane colleagues. She had not even left home for the fall semester when Katrina struck and abruptly cancelled her academic term.

The tears of the diaspora continued with Kristen Barber who sobbed as she told how even the most common things in life—like being able to withdraw money from a bank to pay bills—had been taken away by the storm, and how her efforts to continue graduate school in Michigan were almost sabotaged by this experience of being stripped bare of the most taken for granted necessities.

Jessica Pardee cried as she spoke of how her sociology dissertation had been interrupted twice, once when the federal government shut down a housing project whose residents she had prepared to study, and then again by Katrina. Andrea Wilbon to her credit held together emotionally, and told a riveting tale of the overt racism that she experience as an African American after the storm.

Now it was my turn. Would I hold my emotions in check? Despite being the old guy on the panel and attending sociology conferences and giving presentations for 33 years, I wasn't sure. A cool exterior successfully masked the internal turmoil as I pondered what exactly to say and how to say it.

I began by telling how we were just getting to know the 200 plus evacuated students from New Orleans when the unthinkable happened. On September 22, the city of Lake Charles was ordered evacuated as Hurricane Rita approached. Two days later, Rita slammed into southwest Louisiana, and it would be 16 days before people could return and about three more weeks until school started again at McNeese State. School did eventually resume, and after adding longer class periods and making other adjustments, graduation was held on December 23rd. A few of the New Orleans seniors graduated that night.

Following this "big picture" overview, I went back to parts of my story to fill in some of the details of the sordid ordeal. Unexpectedly, my emotions got the better of me as I described the day before the evacuation was ordered. By that afternoon the New Orleans students were noticeably and very conspicuously absent on the Lake Charles campus. Having been through hell once, they were not waiting around to see their newest home be shattered by yet another hurricane. My voice cracked as I told of the New Orleans students that never returned to Lake Charles after Rita. I pledged that I would personally follow up with these students and would encourage them to continue their educations. Emotions now showing, I muttered a quick conclusion and bowed out to preserve time for the other speakers. Thankfully, I was close to the end anyway, and the audience did not miss much. I was about to conclude with a statement about how proud I had been of the displaced students, especially the seniors, and about how the students felt they had been personally strengthened by the prolonged adversity they experienced.

Next up, and very suddenly thrust into his presentation by my emotional exit, Tim Haney channeled his emotions in another way: he spoke eloquently of the bureaucratic nightmares facing New Orleanians upon their return. They faced surly bill collectors completely unsympathetic with their circumstances; insurance companies that would not pay for damages caused by the storm (the wind vs. water controversy); and hundreds of FEMA trailers sitting unused in an Arkansas field. Tim was very critical of this situation and it was perfectly clear from his presentation that no human being in a civil society should ever have to endure such circumstances, a point warmly embraced by panelists and audience members alike.

Jennifer Day complained of the "masculinization of space" after Katrina; how it had been invaded by Latino construction workers, just about exclusively male, who objectified her in a way she wasn't accustomed to. She strongly suspects that in this more masculinized environment the rates of domestic violence in New Orleans increased after Katrina.

Dr. April Brayfield anchored the panel, her voice lowering and then stopping for a moment as she composed herself. In an intentionally nonlinear expression of her life after Katrina, she mused about her street, her neighbors, FEMA, and her school. Slides of her gutted out, moldly home and the attendant debris piled high on the street outside her home personalized the storm for everyone present.

About 60 people attended the session. I have never witnessed such an attentive or emotional audience at any sociological conference, some crying while we spoke. More than one person praised our courage and encouraged us to put together a paper and perhaps even a monograph of our stories.[4]

When it was all over, I have to say that I was never so glad to escape an academic panel session. Not that I disliked the panel or the people on it, I just wanted to escape once and for all the horrendous pain that I felt in that conference room.[5] It was something I have never experienced in 33 years of sociology meetings, and I hope that I never it experience again. Afterwards, I wandered the streets of the French Quarter aimlessly, glad to be free from all the emotional pain. My legs carried me forward with no particular plan except to walk deep into the French Quarter, as far away as I could from the conference hotel. In this solitary, unplanned journey I did make note of any of my old favorite coffee houses that I stumbled upon. Several of the old haunts had not reopened since the storm; a few others were closed but new construction was a pleasant sign that they would someday come back. I also noted that, while New Orleans did not turn out to be "the city without people," it was definitely a place with few people, far fewer than I ever remember seeing there on all of my previous trips. I wondered on this day if the city would ever get back to the way it used to be.

Traveling back to Lake Charles, tears of diaspora rolled down my cheeks. Though I am an old man who typically takes pride in keeping his emotions under control, I cried for Tulane and New Orleans, for the students doubly displaced by Katrina and Rita, and for myself. I had now seen the devastation of both storms, and where the unspeakable had started for my displaced students. What my New Orleans students had endured was now a part of me.

NOTES

1. One of my students in the Spring of 2006 was a Louisiana State Trooper who had been assigned to work in New Orleans after Katrina. This admonition to stay safe in New Orleans and not venture out very far at night came from this man who understood all too well the dangers.

2. Foucault, *ibid*; Haney, *ibid*.

3. See Ronald Berger and Richard Quinney, *Storytelling Sociology: Narrative as Social Inquiry*. Boulder, CO: Lynne Riener Publishers, 2005.

4. Barber, Hidalgo, Haney, Weeber, Pardee, and Day, *ibid*; Hidalgo and Barber, *ibid*.

5. The Tulane graduate students and faculty were among the most gracious and kind people that I've ever met in my life. I want to emphasize once again that I was not running from them once the session concluded.

Chapter 5

Remembering Sabine Pass

Even if people forget that Hurricane Rita made landfall near Sabine Pass, Texas in September of 2005—and they probably already have—history still provides much to remember about this small town that is the southeastern most place in the state of Texas.

Historical markers in the town note that the first settlers in the area arrived in 1832. The next year, Sam Houston assisted Nachogdoches politician Manuel de los Santos Coy in acquiring a land grant. On January 19, 1839, General Houston signed the charter that established the city of Sabine. Houston was active in promoting the sale of 2,060 town lots, and the city soon flourished, developing into a major port. In 1860 the State Legislature approved a new charter for the city and changed its name to Sabine Pass.

The town was the scene of a memorable major Civil War engagement, the Battle of Sabine Pass, in September, 1863 with Confederate forces preventing a Union attempt to capture the port and gain major inroads into Texas. It was one of the most lopsided victories in naval history. Fewer than 50 Confederate troops led by Lieutenant Richard W. Dowling repulsed a fleet seeking to land up to 15,000 Federal soldiers. Dowling's company, mostly Irishmen from Galveston and Houston, had been comrades in arms since February 1861. Sabine Pass was a strategic center for blockade-running whereby the Confederacy exported cotton and obtained in exchange vital goods such as medicines and arms. Here Dowling's company built Fort Griffin, named in honor of Lieutenant Colonel W. H. Griffin, the Confederate commander at Sabine City. The fort was earthwork strengthened with railroad iron and ship's timbers, and amazingly it was unfinished when the Confederates learned of the approach of 22 ships. Dowling kept watch, but ordered no response to the early shelling by the Federals. When the first ships entered range of Fort Griffin's guns, however, the battle began. Dowling himself served as one of the gunners. The fort sent 137 shells toward the targets.

Several books and research monographs have been written about what transpired during the battle, each highlighting different aspects although converging on certain themes.[1] One is that the Irish Confederates were skillful fighters, taking advantage of their knowledge of the tricky terrain in Sabine Pass. A second theme was the blundering of the Union troops, who needed to station only one ship north of the fort to begin a broadside assault that would have most likely ended in a Union victory.

The following basic facts of the battle are noted in the town's historical markers: Dowling and his troops held off the Union gunboats advancing up the pass. The U.S.S. Clifton and the U.S.S. Arizona ran aground early in the battle. The Clifton and the U.S.S. Sachem both surrendered when disabled by cannon fire. After the battle, more than 300 Federal troops became prisoners of war. Others were killed or missing; many of those had been aboard the Sachem when its boiler exploded as a result of a direct hit on the ship.

After the war the town grew as the Federal Harbor Act of 1882 led to construction of jetties and the development of inland ports along the Neches and Sabine rivers. In October 1886, Sabine Pass was the second largest town in Jefferson County, boasting a new rail line and an optimistic outlook on continued growth as a major coastal port.

On the afternoon of October 12 that year, just two months after a hurricane had destroyed the Texas port of Indianola, a fierce storm ravaged the town of Sabine Pass. The hurricane's 100 mile-per-hour winds and the swiftly rising water swept homes off their foundations and carried people and animals as far as 25 miles away. Eighty-six people, including entire families, were killed, and only two of 77 houses remained intact after the waters subsided. Stories of survival have been documented by historians, signifying the determination of residents to endure the storm. Rescue and cleanup efforts began promptly, with the citizens of Beaumont, Orange, Galveston and Houston providing boats, rescue teams and financial assistance. Special legislative action provided tax relief for the storm ravaged area, exempting citizens from payment of state and county taxes in 1886. As one of several difficulties Sabine Pass faced in the late 19th and early 20th centuries, the 1886 hurricane contributed significantly to the town's decline in the years to come as railway maintenance proved difficult.

The strategic Sabine Pass emerged once again as an important defense base during the Spanish-American War. As tension mounted between the United

States and Spain during the late 1890s, U. S. Representative Samuel Bronson Cooper of Texas recommended the War Department begin plans for the defense of the Pass. Major James B. Quinn of the Army Corps of Engineers in New Orleans was authorized to direct construction of two forts on land granted by Augustus F. Kountze. Work on the batteries was under way by May 1898, one month after the formal war declaration. Military efforts were coordinated with area residents by government engineer J. L. Brownlee. Although the emplacements were soon completed, the shore guns were never part of military action at the Pass.

The natural topography of Sabine Pass became one of the primary points of defense along the Gulf Coast during World War II. In 1941, the U.S. Navy established a Harbor Entrance Control Post (HECP) at the Pass to provide defenses against potential enemy activity in the area. Soon after, the U.S. Army installed artillery emplacements at Texas Point, about 3 and one half miles to the south, that included two 155mm Howitzer guns on Panama mounts, as well as four munitions magazines at this site. The Army's lease of land at Sabine Pass resulted in the location of a temporary harbor defense unit manned by the 256th Coastal Artillery Regiment at Texas Point. Other elements of the defense system included two base end stations, an observation tower, signal stations, large coastal searchlights, a battery commander post and part of the Coast Guard lifeboat station. The munitions magazines also held other ordnance for area installations. Working together, the HECP and the Army post utilized these storage magazines to service the war effort.

Sabine Pass has suffered an unfortunate string of experiences with hurricanes that made landfall in or nearby the town. In addition to the hurricane of 1866 that greatly affected the town's growth as a rail center, storms blew through in 1900, 1915, 1957, and 2005. Audrey, which hit nearby Cameron, Louisiana in 1957, was the final straw in breaking Sabine Pass' quest for economic development. As a result of Audrey, development moved north to the cities of Beaumont, Port Arthur, and Orange, which still dominate the area's economy today.

Sabine Pass' colorful history continued in 1959 when a native son and musician, J.P. "Big Bopper" Richardson died in an Iowa plane crash which became the story line for Don McLean's 1971 classic song, *American Pie.*[2]

The last of the hurricanes to hit was Hurricane Rita in 2005. Rita appeared early on to be a Category 5 monster that could totally and perhaps permanently erase the city of Sabine Pass. Fortunately for the people of the town, the hurricane weakened to Category 3 before hitting them head on. Still, ninety percent of the buildings in the town experienced some kind of damage.

My own field trip to this remarkable place was in early June, 2006, over nine months after Rita struck. I was interested in finding out if this history enriched place would be able to rise yet again from the ravages of a horrific and devastating storm.

Entering from the north on Texas 87, the scene was grim. Businesses on both sides of the road were completely destroyed and appeared to me as if the storm had just passed. An exception, standing out as a gem among ruins was the sparkling new Fire Station #4, which had been refurbished by an *Extreme Makeover* crew.

At the center of town at the intersection of highways 87 and 3322, there were signs of life. Someone had purchased a soft drink machine and placed it on his porch, and the place appeared to be an impromptu community center after the storm. A restaurant nearby had reopened. Across the street, the softball field was repaired and a crowd gathered to see a game.

Further west on 87, on the old road to Galveston, repairs to gravesites rearranged by Rita were underway at the Confederate cemetery. Further down the road on 87, some new dwellings stood out among the others that were in various stages of repair. Sea Rim State Park was still closed, a reminder of the ferocity of Rita's winds. At the McFaddin National Wildlife Refuge, the occasional remnants of boats that washed ashore were the only remaining outward signs of the hurricane.

Turning around and heading east back into town, I returned to the major intersection. Heading right on to 3322, I went south to the historical park near Fort Griffin. The park was closed but that did not stop me from jumping over the orange fences, taking in the scene, and imagining how the Battle of Sabine Pass might have played out in real time. Much of the information about the town and the battle that was shared earlier was obtained from historical markers within the park. It appeared to me that, possibly, the Pass was now wider and deeper than it had been in 1863, judging from the drawings in the historical monographs that I consulted. This means that the Battle, had it been fought today, could have had a much different outcome.

Going north back into town, I turned right at the main intersection on to Broadway. Ahead was the most impressive part of the Sabine Pass "skyline," the offshore oil rig that was being built in the waters of the Pass just east of town. On the way out to look at it, the neighborhood looked much like the one on Highway 87 headed west toward Galveston: some buildings totally repaired, others in various states of repair.

I am completely confident that the town of Sabine Pass will come back. It is the place that has written the book on resiliency, having come back from four previous hurricanes. Rita is just another storm for the hearty souls here to conquer. There is much here worth remembering, not just about Rita but about the area's rich past. I can only hope that future historians will tell fewer stories of conflicts with people and with nature, and more about the remarkable spirit of determination and triumph in this tiny place, and how it thrived despite the long odds against it.

NOTES

1. See for example Frank X. Tolbert, *Dick Dowling at Sabine Pass*. New York: McGraw-Hill, 1962; Edward T. Cotham, *Sabine Pass: the Confederacy's Thermopylae*. Austin, TX: University of Texas Press, 2004.

2. Larry Lehmer, *The Day the Music Died: the Last Tour of Buddy Holly, the Big Bopper, and Ritchie Valens.* New York: Schirmer Books, 1997.

Chapter 6

Remembering Cameron Parish

Louis Cataldie, the East Baton Rouge Parish Coroner who became Louisiana's State Medical Examiner after Hurricane Katrina, opens his memoir a month after Katrina struck New Orleans. In a brief introduction that probably surprised some readers, he writes not of Katrina but of Rita. And he speaks not of New Orleans, but of Cameron.[1]

As the book begins, he is touring Cameron Parish by reconnaissance helicopter. There is no parish to observe, actually; only faint skeletons of what were homes rising like matchsticks from the water—a landscape so desolate and eerie, yet stretching as far as the eye can see. The first person he encounters on the ground is Army Lieutenant General Russel Honore, appointed by President Bush to clean up the Katrina mess and bring order to chaos. Honore uses a military term, "destroyed," to refer to Cameron Parish.[2]

Cataldie and Honore left boot prints on the ground in Cameron Parish, seeing first hand just how bad it was. Lake Charles Mayor Randy Roach knew, too, and so when the national media hovered over his Calcasieu Parish town 40 miles north of Cameron after Hurricane Rita, Roach told the media about what was happening in the neighboring parish to the south.[3] The media didn't follow up. And the national public soon forgot, drawn back into Katrina's problems. Cameron Parish was destined to become the forgotten wasteland of the forgotten storm.

Sure, Katrina was definitely the bigger media story: bigger controversy, more people suffering, more people dead, more journalists covering it, more moral outrage over the slow federal response, more fear for the future, more problems that that didn't get fixed and more problems still unfixed, more than three years later. But it was the almighty dollar that runs the corporate news services of America and that dictated the media coverage. New Orleans is a bigger media market.

Katrina is the older, more experienced and more accomplished sister. Rita is the sister accomplished in her own right, but forever lost in the older sister's shadow. Rita is "that other storm" that people remember vaguely but can't remember her name. Rita's biggest problem was that she followed Katrina. After Katrina, no other storms mattered, at least not to the world's media and viewers.

It would be easy to scorn Katrina, except that we know too well the suffering she cast upon New Orleans. We mourn that suffering. And Katrina may have saved Southwest Louisiana from a human catastrophe of unmatched proportions. Most of the residents there evacuated ahead of Rita. For most of September, people saw the horrific pictures from New Orleans on the nightly news, and this was more than enough incentive for them to bail out as Rita approached.

When Rita made landfall along the Texas/Louisiana border on September 24, 2005, it was a Category 3 hurricane with winds in excess of 120 miles per hour pushing a 20 foot storm surge. The devastation it left behind made it the third most expensive natural disaster in U.S. history. The cost of repairing the damage is estimated at $10 billion.[4]

Much of the area hit by Rita is sparsely populated, though rich in natural resources and industrial infrastructure. The coastal region is dotted by small communities built around fishing, shrimping, and offshore oil services. Low lying marshes and agricultural land where farmers grow rice and sugar cane and ranchers raise horses and cattle extend 30 to 40 miles inland.[5]

Rita spread misery from New Orleans to Galveston, Texas, and beyond. Rita's bands re-flooded parts of New Orleans, and sent a high storm surge through Terrebonne and Vermillion parishes as well as Cameron Parish. Approximately two thousand square miles of farmland and marshes was inundated with sea water, killing livestock, ruining crops, and doing indeterminate damage to the soil and the environment. The storm washed away 98 miles of Louisiana wetlands. Houses in Galveston caught fire, as did a bus carrying evacuees headed north on Interstate 45.[6]

Just as the General suggested, Cameron Parish took the largest hit from Rita, and was mostly destroyed. Cameron, the parish seat, was 90 percent destroyed. As Nola Mae Ross noted, the experience of the folks on Marshall Street was fairly typical of what happened there. Several blocks of the street went missing after the storm: just an empty row of empty slabs that nobody can find a use for. In the meantime everyone is asking, where did all the houses and furniture go? Some went into the back marsh and would retrieve an occasional couch, computer or phone. But where did the bricks go? Ross quips: "It's just one of Rita's devious riddles."[7] And that is not all: Creole was 70 percent destroyed and the resort town of Holly Beach was literally wiped off the face of the earth. No houses, dwellings, or businesses of any kind survived Rita's 20 foot storm surge. Only the water tower remains as evidence of the community that once thrived there.

Cameron Parish did indeed suffer the ravages of war. Overall, destruction from Rita was greater in Cameron Parish than in any other parish, and Cameron has been the slowest parish to recover from the storm due to the massive recovery effort necessary to plan, program and rebuild lost infrastructure. According to *The Rita Report* published at McNeese State University, the parish was closed to the public until June, 2006 as hazardous debris was removed and essential services restored. These tasks were slowed by a lack of basic services and housing for recovery workers. The desire for improved levee and flood control, more stringent building codes and the high cost of insurance have stymied many residents who have been anxious to return and rebuild their communities.[8]

For those that have come back, they are quiet, stoic in the face of tragedy. In their dignified manner, the citizens picked themselves up by the bootstraps and tended to their own affairs. In a manner completely American, they didn't wait for others to act. They took matters into their own hands. They did things the peaceful way. As E.J. Gaspard wrote, no one had to call in the National Guard to restore order. Nobody took a shot at people who came to help, and nobody is asking for a handout. These are people used to hard work. It is Cameron's way of doing things.[9]

Strong families and a sense of community and self sufficiency have a long history, long roots in the low lying soil along the coast. A middle school student wrote after the storm: "We all know each other and know each others' families. Neighbors are your family. Everyone knows everyone. Everyone watches out for everyone."[10]

For some of the elders of these strong extended families, this was the second time that they had seen destruction. On June 27, 1957, another catastrophic storm named Audrey slammed ashore killing 425 people in Cameron Parish. The reason for so many deaths in 1957 was because the weather warning system was new and quite primitive. The Cameron residents had been warned to leave the next day, June 28, so they packed their cars, ready to leave by daylight. But by then, the storm had already hit, and many victims had already lost their homes and their lives, as the giant water surge of up to 30 feet set them sailing out into the marshes to the north.[11]

Lines of communication opened up quickly after Rita, something that didn't happen after Audrey. Within a week of Rita, Cameron Telephone, a wholly owned subsidiary of Cameron Communications had reestablished phone and internet services to the Cameron Courthouse, which housed the Parish emergency operations center. Cameron had power on November 11 and all remaining areas of the parish had power by the end of the year.[12]

The size of the cleanup task was enormous: by one estimate, the debris removed would fill 2,050,000 trash trucks which, if placed end to end and side by side, would fill a four-lane highway from New York to California. By September, 2006 FEMA reported that they had hauled nearly 99 percent of the Rita debris away.[13]

Planning for the future goes forward. *The Rita Report* states that various projects aimed at strengthening the tourism, maritime and commercial fishing sectors are now being considered so that conventional and nontraditional funding sources can be pursued.[14]

On the ground, progress is sluggish. Three years after the storm, the Hurricane Café in Cameron and Sha Sha's Restaurant in Creole were among the few eating spots open for business. No one complains about the slow recovery. But one local writer had this cogent thought: "our tax dollars are funding construction of hospitals and schools in Iraq right now. Cameron Parish deserves at least the same consideration."[15]

On the first anniversary of the storm, a star-studded group of public officials mounted horses for a cattle drive through Cameron Parish that was supposed to put the eyes of the nation upon the plight of Cameron and the need for more funds to expedite the recovery there. Governor Kathleen Blanco, Lt. Governor Mitch Landrieu, U.S. Senators Mary Landrieu and David Vitter, Lt. General Honore, and Don Powell, the Bush administration's coordinator of Gulf Coast rebuilding, all donned the proper attire and rode along in the cattle drive.[16] The show of support by so many important officials was deeply appreciated in the parish. The problem with this story was that only Southwest Louisianans saw it. The national media was transfixed by developments further to the east—the reopening of the Louisiana Superdome on September 25th. Comparisons between the two sisters were about to be made, and in this beauty contest there could only be one winner. The Saints 23-3 victory over Atlanta, and what it meant symbolically to New Orleans' recovery, was the story of the day, hands down.[17] Folks in Cameron could only shake their heads. The older sister had won out once again.

NOTES

1. Louis Cataldie, *Coroner's Journal: Forensics and the Art of Stalking Death.* New York: Berkeley Books, 2007, pp. 4-7.
2. *Ibid.*
3. Brad Goins, "Post Rita Impressions." *Lagniappe*, October 20, 2005, pp. 4-5; see also Goins, "Hurricane Notebook." *Lagniappe*, October 20, 2005, pp. 16-17.
4. Michael Kurth and Daryl Burckel. *The Rita Report.* Baton Rouge, LA: Louisiana Recovery Authority, 2006, p. 8 (hereafter, *The Rita Report*).
5. *Ibid.*
6. *Ibid.*, p. 9.

7. Nola Mae Ross, *The Devastation of Hurricane Rita*. Lake Charles, LA: N.M. Ross, 2006, p. 45.

8. *The Rita Report*, p. 28.

9. E.J. Gaspard, "Ritaville." *Lagniappe*, June 1, 2006, p. 29.

10. Exhibit of photographs and commentaries of Cameron Parish school children after Hurricane Rita, McNeese State University Library, 2006.

11. Fogleman, *ibid.*

12. *The Rita Report*, p. 30.

13. *Ibid.*, p. 16.

14. *Ibid.*, p. 29.

15. Rocke Fournet, "Treat Cameron Parish at Least as Well as We Treat Iraq." *Lagniappe,* May 4, 2006, p. 45.

16. Doug Simpson, "Hundreds in Louisiana Observe One Year Anniversary of Hurricane Rita." *Associated Press*, September 25, 2006.

17. "Saints Crush Falcons in Superdome Return." *Associated Press*, September 26, 2006.

Chapter 7

Remembering Holly Beach

"Destroyed."

"Total, 100 percent devastation."

"It's indescribable."

" For those that want to know what it looks like … it's horrible—you won't be able to find your property."

"I have pain in my heart … "

Such were the descriptions of Holly Beach, Louisiana in late September, 2005 after it had been completely washed away by Hurricane Rita.[1] In the early morning of September 24, a twenty foot storm surge on the northeast eye wall of Rita sent the town in splintered pieces into the marsh about 4 miles to the north. The damage was so complete that one couple that lived in the town for 54 years could not even locate the spot where their home once stood.[2] That's hard for us to grasp, and it's difficult for us to imagine what that kind of overwhelming damage would look like. And the fact that this family could not find their former home in a small town of 300 people where the locals knew every inch of the place since it was rebuilt after Hurricane Audrey is something that almost defies belief: that is, until you see it for yourself.

My colleague Fred Featherstone and I made multiple trips to the beach to see the situation there first hand during 2006.[3] On one trip, Fred found a family that had decided to return. "Yes, we'll rebuild .... This is the only home we've ever known."[4] This was the second time that the family had to build from scratch, the very same plot of land was decimated by Audrey in 1957.

Going through the pain of having your whole town destroyed is something that few, thankfully, will ever have to face. Small towns have been completely destroyed in tornadoes, such as Greensberg, Kansas and perhaps people who are rebuilding after such a tragedy would be able to feel the emotions that Holly Beach residents now feel. Or maybe people in bombed out portions of Baghdad whose homes were reduced to piles of rubble by Iraqi insurgents.

Fortunately it is something that rarely occurs; even the crushed cities of Hiroshima and Nagasaki had some buildings left, some scant shell of infrastructure from which to start rebuilding. The same is true of New Orleans: sad as the situation was there after Katrina, there were parts of the town that remained above water that served as the beginning of the town's rebuilding and revitalization.

At Holly Beach, all that remained were piles of debris that appeared to be randomly tossed about and scattered, and huge piles of sand that blocked the access roads to the beach. A few former utility poles were bent at awkward angles, but managed to survive the storm surge. The only structure that was recognizable after the storm was the water tower on the north edge of town. It was impossible, just as the locals told the press, to gauge where exactly the popular fishing camps once stood or where the Catholic Church, the General Store, the motel and other businesses were once located.

What is most heartbreaking about Holly Beach is the complete wiping away of the entire community that once thrived there. The popular resort town, called the "Cajun Riviera," was close to the hearts of many in southwestern Louisiana. It was one of the few semi developed places on a long coastline that was mostly undeveloped, and that was how the people here wanted it. Even after Rita, the coastline has a raw beauty that is much too scenic to defile with casinos, hotels, shopping malls, and movie theatres.[5]

The future of Holly Beach and that most any town resides with the inclinations of its young people. On balance, the youngsters we spoke with in the rebuilding town seem less willing than their parents and grandparents to come back should another storm hit. "No, I won't be back, I'll be going to Lafayette," is what an 18 year old told Featherstone outside of the trailer that temporarily houses Meaux's Seafood.[6] Such was the cumulative effects of the devastation wrought and the pain in the heart at having to rebuild from scratch.

What's gut wrenchingly hard for people like myself who were frequent visitors to Holly Beach before the storm is the pain of juxtaposing the complete devastation that you see at this place in 2005 or 2006 with all the good memories of time spent here in the past. To me, the pain of looking at Holly Beach in its destroyed state was almost unbearable when I compared it to the happier days that my family had experienced there. In one flashback to October, 2003, I remembered how my extended family, the Featherstones, had come to Lake Charles for one of their many reunions. Though late in October, the weather was still tolerable for going to the beach and enjoying the full range of activities there, and without the crowds we had seen in the summertime. We enjoyed ourselves immensely, stopping at the General Store for refreshments and to buy trinkets that would serve as mementoes of the visit. Looking at the trinkets now brings only tears, as this was the last time any of the Featherstones saw Holly Beach until Fred returned in April, 2006.

In 2008, the pain of diaspora is etched in the faces of the families that have returned. They stare suspiciously at strangers. The figurative "welcome mat," that sense of hospitality that used to be there no longer exists. Tourists and visitors are returning slowly, more each month, perhaps more to gauge the progress of the town than to recreate there. Seeing and witnessing all of this first hand is just about too painful to put into words.

NOTES

1. These quotes were from wire service and television reports during late September and early October of 2005.

2. *Ibid.*

3. This is the relative that figured prominently in my family's evacuation story: see Chapter 1.

4. These trips were taken from April to June 2006.

5. Featherstone interview of April, 2006.

6. Featherstone interview of June, 2006.

Chapter 8

Social Policy and the 2005 Louisiana Hurricanes

I managed to stay in touch with the friends I had met at the memorable 2006 meetings of the Southern Sociological Society in New Orleans. We agreed to work on a paper together as well as a book project, just as people in the audience had urged us to do. As of May, 2008, I am pleased to report that both projects are now thankfully completed.

The pain of the disapora, so apparent to anyone that attended the session, proved so overwhelming that several panel members had to leave Louisiana after Katrina. Kristen Barber and Danielle Hidalgo fled to California, Tim Haney relocated to Oregon and Jessica Pardee to Florida. Andrea Wilbon, Jennifer Day, April Brayfield and I remained in Louisiana, though I lived about three hours away from the others. Undaunted by the distances separating us, the group continued to stay in touch electronically in order to work on the two projects.[1]

Once most of the raw emotion of our situations had passed, we hoped to tell our stories and to do so in a way that could prompt or suggest certain lines of new social policy that could cope with the real life experiences of evacuees: that is the paper project. In the book length project, we attempt to connect our experiences to sociological theory as we had come to know it from our graduate studies onward.

While working on the paper, our individual personalities interacted with the storms we weathered to produce our own unique remembrances and our own cognitions of what was important and what wasn't in the evacuee experience. In my case, I felt an attachment to place that was so strong that I did not want to leave. It was only the social pressure exerted by family and friends that finally convinced me that I must leave Lake Charles ahead of Rita in September, 2005.

Jessica Pardee experienced a profound sense of complacency at several levels, first, in the lackadaisical attitude toward evacuating that she saw in New Orleans. Then, secondly in the slowness of the recovery and in the uncaring attitudes and lack of understanding that she encountered as she traveled outside Louisiana. Kristen Barber, in an experience similar to Jessica's, was treated badly in her hometown. Born and raised in Michigan, by 2005 she was an outsider, a New Orleanian, a stranger, an evacuee, an "other." This "stranger at home" experience was an odd twist on Simmel's classic stranger that she found to be greatly distasteful.

Tim Haney and his family was treated horribly and with great incompetence by social service workers he encountered in south Louisiana. Jessica Day was one of the first in our panel to return to New Orleans and complained of the "masculination of space" she encountered there as she was objectified by male recovery workers.

Six themes emerged from our stories that have implications for social policy: 1) displacement and attachment to place; 2) blasé attitudes of unattached "host" communities; 3) protocol of bureaucratic agencies; 4) the masculine worker ideal and its relationship to emotional management, role conflict, and alienation; 5) spatial dynamics of disaster zones and its implication for gender and sexual rights; and 6) ongoing struggles with the above topics. These themes are discussed along with corresponding sets of policy recommendations below.[2]

In Louisiana, there is a strong sense of place and belonging to a community that is difficult for people outside the south or outside the Gulf Coast to understand.[3] Heritage based personal narratives may be laced with portions that state that "no member of my family has ever evacuated," or "we don't have many hurricanes here." I had to navigate through such historical narratives as I pondered a decision about evacuation. I had lived in Lake Charles long enough to have a longing to stay when Rita arrived, and understood completely where those people were coming from that did not want to leave. It was an obstacle I had to overcome. Eventually I tapped a vein of social capital that I had built up in the community. My landlord insisted that I evacuate. I met this person through a voluntary association, and would eventually be related to him because the landlord's brother would become engaged to my niece. My social network and extended family actually made the decision for me: I was leaving whether I wanted to go or not. The lack of such social ties, or living alone, has been associated with decisions not to evacuate oncoming disasters such as the Chicago

heat wave of 1995.[4] Had I been a bachelor, there's no way I would have evacuated.

Given the city's unique history and cultural traditions, New Orleanians faced
probably an even deeper connection to place along with a long dose of what
Jessica Pardee (and Simmel) called a blasé attitude toward evacuation that contributed to a culture of complacency around the oncoming storm. While the
blasé attitude helped Jessica to remain calm during the evacuation and to con-
ceptualize the storm as a problem that needed to be solved or fixed, for others it
just fed a basic cultural complacency about storms that contributed to the deaths
of over 1,300 New Orleanians during and after the hurricane.

The blasé attitude was evident as well in most of the "host" communities that
the sociologists found themselves in when they evacuated. Jessica Pardee
pointed out how people she encountered in Texas and South Carolina found it
difficult to identify with her plight, some being completely indifferent to her
situation while others assigned her a deviant label that left her character and
reputation spoiled or besmirched.[5] Perhaps worse, Kristen Barber encountered a
few Michiganders that told her that she was to blame for her own problems because she voluntarily chose to live below sea level in New Orleans.

The protocol of bureaucratic agencies some of the evacuees faced was inadequate, ineffective, and uncaring. The officials entrusted to provide aid were
blasé to the evacuees' plight, as Jessica and Tim aptly noted. In a bureaucratized
world of social benefits, empathy, love, and caring are disvalued characteristics.
The treatment that Tim Haney and Jessica Pardee faced was thus normal given
the application of "rational" bureaucratic norms to the situation that they found
themselves in: hungry, depleted, desperately in need of help, and tired of waiting
for results. I would have to say that my own positive experience in Farmerville
ran counter to that of the other panelists.

One of the policy implications that emerge from our first three themes is that
mandatory evacuation orders need to be issued much earlier than in the past. For
Katrina, the orders emerged about one day before the storm's landfall. It is recommended that orders be issued much earlier, perhaps as early as 72 hours before landfall, so that people with inhibitions about leaving can have those inhibitions sufficiently broken down. The warnings should be accompanied by public
education, specifically the National Weather Service's prognosis of likely damage to areas at landfall. The warnings and public information should be repeated
at regular intervals, for example, every six hours, to continue to chip away at
whatever barriers locals may have constructed so as not to leave. A longer term
recommendation is to encourage the buildup of social capital in local communities. The richer the line of social capital and the longer one has to tap it, the
more likely that people may use a resource from their social network in order to
evacuate. Robbins, commenting on how social capital can be built up in areas
where it has been depleted due to globalization, recommends the following:
buyback of resources by the local community from global corporations such as
urban land spaces, farms, local media, and local banks; and increased involve-
ment in voluntary organizations such as sports teams, shared community spaces,
local theatre, community centers, and school boards.[6]

We also recommend that community centers be opened, first outside the damage zone and later inside, to serve as triage centers that would supplement but not replace the Red Cross shelters that were a shelter of last resort for many fleeing Hurricane Katrina. These centers would provide virtual (i.e., internet) and physical spaces where evacuees can interact with and discuss their experiences and options with other evacuees and people with similar experiences. Based on our stories and information from local non-governmental organizations in New Orleans, "information" and access to information was a major problem for residents of affected areas. Residents of affected areas have a right to know what all of their options are in the event of a major disaster. Internet and free hotlines should make this information available. Further, the government should provide residents with spaces throughout the United States where they can receive this information and discuss their experiences and options with other affected people. As expressed in our narratives, the need for interaction with those who are experiencing the same issues is important in deflecting feelings of alienation and isolation. We know this not only from Katrina and Rita but from history: the failure of HUD to establish community centers after the Buffalo Creek flood left survivors frozen in a moment of extreme dislocation that lasted more than a year.[7]

Universities and colleges might be pressed into service as triage centers if local communities are unwilling or unable to provide assistance. Such institutions are cosmopolitan, culturally diverse, and filled with people of different backgrounds with unique life experiences. As Jessica found out, sociological colleagues at the University of Central Florida understood her situation completely—they too had suffered social dislocations in the aftermath of hurricanes during 2004. Such institutions, additionally, might have links to the therapeutic and mental health community that evacuees desperately need. Kristen Barber, while in Michigan, was in mourning for the life that she had lost, and indeed everyone who experiences disasters such as Katrina or Rita experience some form of emotional and psychological trauma, ranging from shock and confusion, to disbelief, anger, and depression. Additionally, emotional and psychological assistance may be needed by those whose present compromised mental state (in the aftermath of the event) arises out of experiences of role conflict, the blasé attitude, and bureaucratic state help gone awry, all of which were mentioned in our stories. Information needs to be made readily available to the public; phone numbers of "stress" help hotlines, much like suicide and domestic violence hotlines, may provide immediate aid, relief, and information for further help. These numbers need to put people into contact with hotline operators who are available twenty-four hours a day, preferably toll-free. These numbers need to be posted on flyers as well as on television, internet, and radio.

The triage centers would also be important sources of information for the locals of the host communities, as locals sometimes feel anxiety and fear with the arrival of evacuees.[8] Especially if official news sources are not operating due to technical problems, rumors often take the place of news, and the rumor process represents the community's best efforts to manufacture news collectively by themselves.[9] The triage centers would allow locals and evacuees to get to know one another and to share information, to build up relationships, and to dispel rumors.

After Katrina and Rita, affected areas lacked both health care and mental health care workers. An effort to recruit these workers back into the area needs to be a priority comparable to that of recruiting construction workers and security officers. An innovative program of the Louisiana Home Care Association to recruit home health workers to Louisiana after Katrina via internet is a model worthy of further study and possibly replication.[10]

It is also clear that bureaucratic institutions must make an effort to be less bureaucratic. Many hurricane evacuees were frustrated and confused by the process of acquiring aid and basic support. While this is hardly unique to the post-Katrina setting this process has to be simplified.[11] As Tim mentioned in his narrative, online information stated that the Department of Family Services was waiving the rules of food stamp application and reception for all those in affected areas. However, the state agency did not make the application process easier, nor did they provide aid for Tim or for his family. Information regarding disaster victims' right to aid needs to be much more widely distributed and made available in forms other than the internet, which not all people have access to. Also, all individual agencies need to be made aware of the situation and the manner in which evacuees are to be assisted. Having protocol systematically drawn-up and briefing all agency employees on the processes that must be followed in order to deal with such an emergency will surely help. At the same time, mechanisms must be put in place that addresses the individual concerns and questions of those affected by disaster. We suggest a more effective internet-based and telephone process that allows individuals to discuss their individual situations with agents.

A fourth theme that emerged from the narrative is the masculine worker ideal and its relationship to emotional management, role conflict, and alienation. For those that returned to the city early, New Orleans was a highly masculinized space of male military police and construction workers, some blatantly hostile to women in their stark displays of street sexual harassment. Jennifer Day found her new home space so highly sexualized that others were now interpreting her as a vulnerable and exposed feminine body. Warned to stay inside, she did, at least at night; the rest of the time she defiantly insisted that this was her home and that she had a right to be there. Thus, hope for the future was intermixed with fear, frustration, sorrow, and anger for what her city had become.

A fifth theme, closely related and intertwined with the fourth, is the spatial dynamics of disaster zones and its implication for gender and sexual rights. The end result of Jennifer Day's experience was a feeling that she was a prisoner in her own home. The masculinized city she came back to was a controlling place, dominated by men who limited her personal right to freedom of expression and freedom of assembly in just about every aspect of her life: socially, economically, politically, educationally, and emotionally. This experience was by no means unique to New Orleans after Katrina; a similar masculization of space and corresponding discounting of female roles and female labor occurred after the Red River flood of 1997 and the Oakland-Berkeley Hills fires of 1991.[12]

The final theme is the ongoing struggles with each of the preceding themes. The physical and emotional exhaustion of dealing with the above issues did not end, because the "new normal" was a constant reminder of what happened to each of the sociologists and how much further their lives would have to progress before they resembled in any way how things used to be. The new normal involves reliving past traumas. Kristen Barber cried during her 2006 SSS presentation (as most of us did) while Danielle Hidalgo was conflicted by the anger she felt toward her university and the loyalty she felt for her mentors there.

The final three themes suggest, among other things, that it is important to provide a safe and supportive environment for women who reenter a disaster site that has a majority of men residing there. Jennifer and many other women felt vulnerable and perpetually experienced sexual harassment by men, assault, and the violation of their space and bodies. Such a masculine environment, such as the one that immediately unfolded after Katrina in New Orleans, is threatening to women and inhibits their ability to move about their world as free agents to accomplish even the most mundane activities such as walking to the grocery store. Many small, but important, procedures may be implemented to address the concerns and fears of women returning to a disaster sight.

First, it is suggested that there be ample street lighting in the evenings.[13] Most lampposts and streetlights were severely damaged during Hurricane Katrina and not functional even six months after the storm passed. However, electrically generated lamps may be provided to help alleviate dark alleys and major walkways. Second, free shuttle service should be provided and run regularly both night and day in order to transport women to grocery stores, doctor's offices, home, and so on. At a time when public transportation is not simply at its worse, but rather not working at all, women must have safe, reliable, and quick transportation in order to get from home to a number of basic places. Lastly, emergency street side phones must be available, with posted phone numbers one may call in a number of different emergency situations. These phones would resemble those that are posted along many expressways. The numbers provided would allow women to contact hotlines that could help them in case of domestic abuse, mugging, rape, and other serious threat and harm.

Colleges and universities once again emerge as potential sources of social support for women as they work to make the post disaster city safer. Consortia of university women's studies programs, even if formed ad hoc following disasters, might provide lines of social, emotional, and even financial resources to provide the items that women need to be safe. Women need capable advocates to negotiate successful procurement of the much needed items, and women's studies professors and students may be in a position to help. As bureaucracy may be blasé to their requests, decisive action outside normal bureaucratic channels may be needed to accomplish the goals outlined above.

To conclude, the sociological narratives we constructed are sociological stories. Employing the sociological imagination, our professional and personal lives were merged during our exile from our homes. Amidst the ruin of our lives, the work of some great sociologists provided a language that helped us to better see and perceive what was happening around us. This in turn stimulated ideas about social policy. Additionally, it occurred to us that a relatively new sociological concept, social capital, is one that might be an umbrella concept to guide future work on the transitions to post-disaster life.[14] Social capital was a resource needed in order to evacuate; it was something sorely missed by evacuees "on the road"; and something that needs to be built up once again, or replenished, as evacuees discover and cope with the new normal that lies ahead.

NOTES

1. Panelists Andrea Wilbon and April Brayfield declined to participate in the writing of the paper. Wilbon, however contributed the lead chapter to the book project while Brayfield stayed focused on a research project of several years duration.

2. These policy recommendations were not included in the paper project because the paper had reached the maximum length allowable by the editor.

3. Wilkinson and Ross, *ibid.*

4. Eric Klinenberg, *Heat Wave: A Social Autopsy of Disaster in Chicago.* Chicago: University of Chicago Press, 2002.

5. Becker, ibid; Goffman, 1963.

6. Richard Robbins, *Global Problems and the Culture of Capitalism.* Boston: Allyn and Bacon, 2005; Robert Putnam, *Bowling Alone.* New York: Simon and Schuster, 2000.

7. Kai Erickson, *Everything in its Path: Destruction of Community in the Buffalo Creek Flood.* New York: Simon and Schuster, 1976.

8. Peter Applebome, "In Baton Rouge, A Tinge of Evacuee Backlash." *New York Times,* September 7, 2005.

9. Tamotsu Shibutani, *Improvised News:A Sociological Study of Rumor.* Indianapolis: Bobbs-Merrill, 1966.

10. Stan Weeber, "Home Health Care after Hurricanes Katrina and Rita: A Report from the Field." *Home Health Care Management and Practice,* 19, (2), 2007, pp. 104-111.

11. Bates, *ibid.*

12. Elaine Enarson and Joseph Scanlon, "Gender Patterns in Flood Evacuation: A Case Study in Canada's Red River Valley." *Applied Behavioral Science Review,* 7, 1999, pp. 103-124; S. Hoffman, "Eve and Adam Among the Embers: Gender Patterns after the Oakland Berkeley Firestorm. In Elaine Enarson and Betty Morrow (Eds.), *The Gendered Terrain of Disaster: Through Women's Eyes.* Westport, CT: Praeger, 1998.

13. Jennifer Day, Erica Dudas and Andrea Wilbon, "It's Raining Men: Gendered Environments Post Disaster. Unpublished manuscript, Department of Sociology, Tulane University, 2006.

14. Liesel Ritchie and Duane Gill, *Social Capital and Subsistence in the Wake of the Exxon Valdez Oil Spill.* Mississippi State University: Social Science Research Center, 2004; Jerry Buckland and Matiur Rahman, "Community-Based Disaster Management During the 1997 Red River Flood in Canada. *Disasters,* 23, (2), 1999, pp. 174-192.

Bibliography

Applebome. Peter. 2005. "In Baton Rouge, A Tinge of Evacuee Backlash." *New York Times,* September 7.

Asch, Solomon. 1936. *A Study of Change in Mental Organization.* New York: Archives of Psychology.

Babbie, Earl. 1995. *Adventures in Social Research.* Thousand Oaks, CA: Pine Forge Press.

Babington, Charles. 2005."Hastert Tries Damage Control After Remarks Hit a Nerve." *Washington Post*, September 3: A17.

Baker, George. 1962. *Man and Society in Disaster.* New York: Basic Books.

Barber, Kristen, Danielle Hidalgo, Timothy Haney, Stan Weeber, Jessica Pardee, and Jennifer Day. 2007. "Narrating the Storm: Storytelling as a Methodological Approach to Understanding Hurricane Katrina." *Journal of Public Management and Social Policy*, 13, (2), 99-120.

Barton, Allen. 1969. *Communities in Disaster; A Sociological Analysis of Collective Stress Situations.* New York: Doubleday.

Bates, Frederick. 1963. *The Social and Psychological Consequences of a Natural Disaster: A Longitudinal Study of Hurricane Audrey.* Washington, D.C.: National Academy of Sciences, National Research Council.

Becker, Howard. 1963. *Outsiders.* London: Free Press of Glencoe.

Berger, Ronald and Richard Quinney. 2005. *Storytelling Sociology: Narrative as Social Inquiry.* Boulder, CO: Lynne Rienner Publishers.

Brayfield, April. 2006. 'Ongoing Stories, Ongoing Struggles, " Paper presented at the annual meetings of the Southern Sociological Society, New Orleans, March.

Brookfield, Stephen. 2006. *The Skillful Teacher.* San Francisco: Jossey-Bass.

Brookfield, Stephen. 2005. *The Power of Critical Theory.* San Francisco: Jossey-Bass.

Brookfield, Stephen. 1995. *Becoming a Critically Reflective Teacher.* San Francisco: Jossey-Bass.

Brookfield. Stephen. 1990. *The Skillful Teacher*. San Francisco: Jossey-Bass.

Brookfield, Stephen. 1986. *Understanding and Facilitating Adult Learning*. San Francisco: Jossey-Bass.

Buckland, Jerry and Matiur Rahman. 1999. "Community-Based Disaster Management During the 1997 Red River Flood in Canada. *Disasters*, 23, (2), 174-192

Cataldie, Louis. 2007. *Coroner's Journal: Forensics and the Art of Stalking Death*. New York: Berkeley Books.

Clawson, Dan (Ed.). 2007. *Public Sociology*. Berkeley, CA: University of California Press.

Cotham, Edward. 2004. *Sabine Pass: The Confederacy's Thermopylae*. Austin, TX: University of Texas Press.

Danzig, Elliott, Paul Thayer and Lila Galanter. 1958. "The Effects of a Threatening Rumor on a Disaster Stricken Community." Washington, D.C.: National Academy of Sciences, National Research Council.

Day, Jennifer. 2006. "Harassment on the Streets." Paper presented at the annual meetings of the Southern Sociological Society, New Orleans, March.

Day, Jennifer, Erica Dudas and Andrea Wilbon. 2006. "It's Raining Men: Gendered Environments Post Disaster. Unpublished manuscript, Department of Sociology, Tulane University.

De Sola Pool, Ithiel, Stanley Milgram, Theodore Newcomb and Manfred Kochen. 1989. *The Small World*. Norwood, N.J.: Ablex Publishers.

Dynes, Russell. 1970. *Organized Behavior in Disaster*. Lexington, MA: Heath Lexington Books.

Dyson, Michael. 2006. *Come Hell or High Water: Hurricane Katrina and the Color of Disaster*. New York: Basic Civitas.

Enarson, Elaine and Joseph Scanlon. 1999. "Gender Patterns in Flood Evacuation: A Case Study in Canada's Red River Valley." *Applied Behavioral Science Review*, 7, 103-124.

Erickson, Kai. 1994. *A New Species of Trouble: Explorations in Disaster, Trauma and Community*. New York: W.W. Norton and Company.

Erickson, Kai. 1976. *Everything in its Path: Destruction of Community in the Buffalo Creek Flood*. New York: Simon and Schuster.

Fischer, Henry. 1998. *Response to Disaster: Fact Versus Fiction and its Perpetuation: The Sociology of Disaster*. Lanham, MD: University Press of America.

Fisher, Seymour. 1993. "Personal Interview." University of Texas Medical Branch, Galveston, TX.

Fogleman, Charles. 1958. *A Socio-Psychological Study of the Effects of a Major Disaster Upon Individuals and Groups Within the Impact Area*. Ph.D. Dissertation, Louisiana State University.

Fornet, Rocke. 2006. "Treat Cameron Parish at Least as Well as We Treat Iraq." *Lagniappe*, May 4, 45.

Foucault, Michel. 1977. *Discipline and Punish: the Birth of the Prison*. New York: Pantheon Books.

Fritz, Charles and J.H. Mathewson. 1957. *Convergence Behavior in Disasters; A Problem of Social Control*. Washington, D.C.: National Research Council.

Gaspard. E.J. 2006. "Ritaville." *Lagniappe*, June 1, 29.

Goffman, Erving. 1981. *Forms of Talk*. Philadelphia: University of Pennsylvania Press.

Goffman, Erving. 1974. *Frame Analysis*. New York: Harper and Row.

Goffman, Erving. 1967. *Interaction Ritual*. Garden City, N.Y.: Anchor Books.

Goffman, Erving. 1963. *Stigma*. Englewood Cliffs, N.J.: Prentice Hall.

Goffman, Erving. 1959. *The Presentation of Self in Everyday Life*. Garden City, N.Y.: Doubleday.

Goins, Brad. 2005a. "Post Rita Impressions." *Lagniappe*, October 20, 4-5.

Goins, Brad. 2005b. "Hurricane Notebook." *Lagniappe*, October 20, 16-17.

Gouldner, Alvin. 1970. *The Coming Crisis of Western Sociology*. New York: Basic Books.

Haney, Tim. 2006. "Bureaucatic Issues and Hurricane Katrina." Paper presented at the annual meetings of the Southern Sociological Society, New Orleans, March.

Hart, Lianne, David Zucchino and Jaimes Rainey. 2005. "A City in Survival Mode Restoring Order." *Los Angeles Times*, September 4.

Hidalgo, Danielle Antoinette. 2006. "After Hurricane Katrina: Storytelling Sociology." Paper presented at the annual meetings of the Southern Sociological Society, New Orleans, March.

Hidalgo, Danielle Antoinette and Kristen Barber (Eds.). 2007. *Narrating the Storm: Sociological Stories of Hurricane Katrina*. Newcastle: Cambridge Scholars Press.

Hill, John. 2005. "Baton Rouge: A City Under Stress." *Shreveport Times*, September 2.

Hoffman, S. 1998. "Eve and Adam Among the Embers: Gender Patterns after the Oakland Berkeley Firestorm. In Elaine Enarson and Betty Morrow (Eds.) *The Gendered Terrain of Disaster: Through Women's Eyes*. Westport, CT: Praeger.

Klinenberg. Eric. 2002. *Heat Wave: A Social Autopsy of Disaster in Chicago*. University of Chicago Press.

Kurth, Michael and Daryl Burckel. 2006. *The Rita Report*. Baton Rouge, LA: Louisiana Recovery Authority.

Lehmer, Larry. 1997. *The Day the Music Died: the Last Tour of Buddy Holly, the Big Bopper and Ritchie Valens*. New York: Schirmer Books.

Mangan, Katherine. 2005. "Colleges Hit by Rita Face Major Repairs and an Uncertain Future." *Chronicle of Higher Education*, October 7.

McAdam, Douglas and Gary T. Marx. 1994. *Collective Behavior and Social Movements*. Englewood Cliffs, N.J.: Prentice Hall.

Merton, Robert. 1938. "Social Structure and Anomie." *American Sociological Review*, 3, 672-682.

Milgram, Stanley. 1974. *Obedience to Authority*. New York: HarperPerrenial.

Mills, C. Wright. 1959. *The Sociological Imagination*. New York: Oxford University Press.

Moore, Harry. 1963. *Before the Wind: A Study of the Response to Hurricane Carla*. Washington D.C.: National Research Council.

Moore, Harry. 1958. *Tornadoes Over Texas: A Study of Waco and San Angelo in Disaster*. Austin, TX: University of Texas Press.

Pardee, Jessica. 2006. "Disaster Experiences of Low Income Families Facing Hurricane Katrina." Paper presented at the annual meetings of the Southern Sociological Society, New Orleans, March.

Putnam. Robert. 2000. *Bowling Alone*. New York: Simon and Schuster.

Ritchie, Liesel and Duane Gill. 2004. *Social Capital and Subsistence in the Wake of the Exxon Valdez Oil Spill*. Mississippi State University: Social Science Research Center.

Robbins, Richard. 2005. *Global Problems and the Culture of Capitalism*. Boston: Allyn and Bacon.

Ross, Nola Mae. 2006. The Devastation of Hurricane Rita. Lake Charles, LA: N.M. Ross.

Scurlock, Stephanie. 2006. "Hurricane Sex Offenders Living in Midsouth Neighborhoods." *News 3*, Memphis, Tennessee, March 31.

Shibutani, Tamotsu. 1966. *Improvised News: A Sociological Study of Rumor*. Indianapolis: Bobbs-Merrill.

Simpson, Doug. 2006. 'Hundreds in Louisiana Observe One Year Anniversary of Hurricane Rita." *Associated Press*, September 25.

Tolbert, Frank. 1962. *Dick Dowling at Sabine Pass*. New York: McGraw-Hill.

Turner, Billy M. 2005a. "Memo to the Social Sciences Faculty." McNeese State University, September 4.

Turner, Billy M. 2005b. "Memo to the Social Sciences Faculty." McNeese State University, August 30.

Weeber, Stan. 2007. "Home Health Care after Hurricanes Katrina and Rita: A Report from the Field." *Home Health Care Management and Practice*, 19, (2), 104-111.

Wilkinson, Kenneth and Peggy Ross. 1970. *Citizens' Responses to Warnings of Hurricane Camille*. State College, MS: Social Science Research Center, Mississippi State University.

Index

A

Acadians 19
Alabama National Guard 16
Alex 34,37
Alexandria, Louisiana 6
American Pie 45
American Sociological Review 21,69
Applebome, Peter 65,67
Applied Behavioral Science Review 65,68
Asch, Solomon 21,67

B

Babbie, Earl 21,67
Babington, Charles 38,67
Baker, George 28,67
Barber, Kristen x.,21-22,29,40,42,59-61,
    64,67,69
Barton, Allen 28,67
Bates, Frederick 28,65,67
Baton Rouge, Louisiana 2,12,20,32,69
Battle of Sabine Pass 43-44
Beaumont, Texas 45
Becker, Howard 38,65,67
Belcher, Patti xi.

Berger, Ronald 42,67
Bernice, Louisiana 36
Blanco, Katherine 52
Brayfield, April x.,21,29,41,59,65,67
Brookfield, Stephen 24-25,28,67-68
Brown, Walter xi.
Brownsville, Texas 3
Buckland, Jerry 65,68
Buffalo Creek Flood 62,68
Burckel, Daryl 52,69
Burton Coliseum 2,32

C

Calcasieu Parish, Louisiana 5,9
Cameron, Louisiana vi.,2-3,45,52
Cameron Parish, Louisiana vii.2,5,9,
    20,49,50,53
Cataldie, Louis 49,52,68
Chandra 32-33,35
Chattanooga, Tennessee 20
Cheryse 32,37-38
Chronicle of Higher Education
    10,21,69

L

Lacassine, Louisiana 10
Lagniappe vii.,52,68-69
Lake Charles, Louisiana vii., ix.-xi.,1-
  13,15,20,23,25,31-33,36-37,39-42,
  57,60
Landrieu, Mary 52
Landrieu, Mitch 52
LeCompte, Louisiana 6
Lehmer, Larry 47,69
Louisiana Home Care Association 63
Louisiana State University 28,68
Louisiana Superdome 18,52

M

Mangan, Katherine 21,69
Marx, Gary 21,69
Mathewson, J.H. 28,68
McAdam, Douglas 21,69
McLean, Don 45
McNeese State University x.,2-3,10,
  13,16,18,23-28,32,37-38,51,53
Memphis, Tennessee 21,69
Merton, Robert 21,69
Miami, Florida 3
Michelle 35
Miles, Ray x.
Milgram, Stanley 21,36,38,68-69
Mills, C. Wright vi.,21,69
Mississippi State University 29,65,
  69-70
Mizell-Nelson, Michael x.
Moore, Harry 28,69
Monroe, Louisiana 5,6
Morrow, Betty 65,69

N

National Academy of Sciences
  21,28,67-68
National Guard 8,13
National Research Council
  21,28,67-69
National Weather Service 61
Nevada 20
Newcomb, Theodore 38,68

New Iberia, Louisiana 3-4
New Orleans Convention
  Center 18
New Orleans, Louisiana x.,2-
  4,6,11-15,17-19,21,23,27,31-
  38,39-42,49-50, 59-60,62-
  63,69
Northwestern Oklahoma State
  University 3
Nova Scotia 19

O

Oak Grove, Louisiana vi.
Oakland-Berkeley Hills Fires
  64-65,69
Orange, Texas 4,45
Orton, Debi x.

P

Pardee, Jessica x.,21,40,42,59-
  62,67,69
Palestinians 19
Port Arthur, Texas 4,45
Port of Lake Charles 17,27
Powell, Don 52
Putnam, Robert 65,69

Q

Quinney, Richard 42

R

Rahman, Matiur 65,68
Rainey, James 21,69
Red River Flood 64-65,68
Richardson, J.P. 45
Rita, Hurricane 1-65
Rita Report 51-53,69
Ritchie, Liesel 65,69
Roach, Randy vii., x.,49
Robbins, Richard 61,65,69
Ross, Nola Mae 50-51,53,69
Ross, Peggy 29,65,70
Rothman, Judith x.

About the Author

Stan C. Weeber (Ph.D., University of North Texas, 2000) is an Associate Professor of Sociology and Criminal Justice at McNeese State University in Lake Charles, Louisiana. His interests in sociology include applied sociology, the sociology of sociology, sociological theory, political sociology, collective behavior and social movements, and crime/deviance. The author of ten books, his sociological work has appeared in *The American Sociologist*, *The Sociological Quarterly*, *Journal of Public Management and Social Policy*, *Contemporary Sociology*, *Canadian Review of Sociology and Anthropology*, *International Review of Modern Sociology*, and several other journals.